D1156349

FLAVORIZE

GREAT MARINADES, INJECTIONS,
BRINES, RUBS, and GLAZES

FLAVORIZE

Ray "Dr. BBQ" Lampe

Foreword by DERRICK RICHES   Photographs by ANGIE MOSIER

CHRONICLE BOOKS
SAN FRANCISCO

ACKNOWLEDGMENTS

Many thanks to Bill LeBlond for all the support over the years. Enjoy your retirement, friend. Thanks to Amy Treadwell for all the hard work and for always making me look so good. Thanks to everyone at Chronicle for doing that thing you do. Thanks to Scott Mendel for always finding the right answer, and, last but not least, thanks to Sandi for putting up with it all and keeping the home fires burning. Oh, and thanks to Minnie Pearl for being so cute.

Text copyright © 2015 by Ray Lampe.
Foreword copyright © 2015 by Derrick Riches.
Photographs copyright © 2015 by Angie Mosier.
All rights reserved. No part of this book may be reproduced in any form without written permission from the publisher.

Library of Congress Cataloging-in-Publication Data:

Lampe, Ray.
  Flavorize : great marinades, injections, brines, rubs, and glazes / Ray "Dr. BBQ" Lampe ; foreword by Derrick Riches ; photographs by Angie Mosier.
    pages cm
  Includes index.
  ISBN 978-1-4521-2530-5 -- ISBN 1-4521-2530-9 1.
  Marinades. 2. Barbecuing. I. Title.

TX819.M26L36 2015
641.81'4--dc23

                    2014014504

ISBN 978-1-4521-2530-5

Manufactured in China

MIX
Paper from responsible sources
FSC® C104723

Designed by Benjamin Shaykin
Typeset in Gin, Circular, Lyon, and Parkinson

BBQ Guru's Digi-Q is a registered trademark of The BBQ Guru; Big Green Egg is a registered trademark of Big Green Egg Inc.; Coca-Cola is a registered trademark of The Coca-Cola Company; Morton's Kosher Salt and Morton's Tender Quick are registered trademarks of Morton International Inc.; Pendery's San Antonio Red Spice is a registered trademark of Pendery's Inc.; Shun knives are registered trademarks of Kai USA Ltd.; Sugar In The Raw is a registered trademark of Cumberland Packing Company; Superfast Thermapen is a registered trademark of ThermoWorks; Vitamix blender is a registered trademark of Vita-Mix Corp.

10 9 8 7 6 5 4 3 2 1

Chronicle Books LLC
680 Second Street
San Francisco, California 94107
www.chroniclebooks.com

Contents

FOREWORD

Cooking is both an art and a science, but infusing with flavor is purely art. In *Flavorize*, Ray Lampe brushes with bold strokes, but that has always been Ray's greatest strength. As a writer in the world of barbecue, I often bump into him at trade shows, food competitions, and a variety of other food events. While I wander these spaces looking for what's new, interesting, or a good story, Ray is usually cooking. I prefer an event I know he will be attending, as it means I have a place to drop my bag, put up my feet, and grab a quick bit to eat. Ray is almost always cooking, and will clue me in when something delicious is ready to come off the grill or out of the smoker.

Hanging out in Ray's event tent has given me ample time to watch him work, but it never seems like work. Dishes come together while he talks with passersby or laughs with friends who are doing pretty much what I am—taking advantage of the shade, the food, and the company. And his cooking always seems effortless. I know few people who can so easily blend flavors together to make something fantastic from whatever there is on hand. I haven't had the chance to watch Ray cook at home, with all his ingredients and kitchen at his disposal, but I imagine that this book is an ample reflection of what it would be like to drop by for dinner.

In the nearly two decades that I have written about barbecue and grilling, I have read a lot of books, and Ray's have consistently been among the best. When I heard he was working on one about marinades, injections, brines, rubs, and glazes, I was skeptical. I've seen these books before and the biggest problem is that as well put together as a marinade recipe might be, if the reader can't see it in action, read about how to apply it, or get a feel for what the flavors are going to be, it doesn't have a lot of value. Once I had the chance to read this book, however, I was immediately relieved.

Flavorize is as much a collection of great recipes as it is a lesson in exceptional cooking. Take Ray's recipe for Cuban Mojo Marinade. The ingredients are fresh, the flavors bold, and it can be prepared in just a few minutes. But Ray doesn't stop with a really good mojo recipe; he goes on to show how he would use it, by marinating some good, thick loin-cut country ribs destined for the grill. By including a detailed example of how each marinade, injection, brine, rub, or glaze might be used, this book takes readers from flavor to plate in a way that expands their own cooking ability and not just their recipe collection.   —*Derrick Riches*

SOAKING, POKING, RUBBING, AND BRUSHING

It's often said that the way to a man's heart is through his stomach.

There is little doubt that this is true—and it seems to work pretty well on women, too. But most of us don't fall for just any ol' good meal. It's the *great* meals that get our attention and provoke our amorous admiration for the cook. As cooks, we all want to prepare that great meal, but how do we do that? What sets a great meal apart from just a good one?

Top-quality meats, seafood, and veggies are a great place to start, but that's pretty simple. You always want to start with great ingredients, so you should always seek them out. Sometimes that means spending a little extra money, and sometimes it just means driving across town to a great market. Either way, it's always recommended.

Achieving the perfect degree of doneness is key to any great food as well. If your food is coming out tough and dry, you're probably overcooking it and no marinade or glaze is going to help. And if it's underdone and raw, well, you can probably figure that one out yourself. Perfect doneness is a tough skill to master, but with a good instant-read thermometer and a lot of attention, we can all learn to become good at it.

But no matter what you buy and how perfectly you cook it, it's the seasoning that can take it from good to great. Achieving great flavors through proper seasoning is what every chef and every home cook strives for, and the ones that get it just right are legendary.

Simple can be good. A great chef friend once told me that the difference between a good meal and a great one was the perfect amount of salt. That might be a little too basic, but it's true that simple ingredients can be great. The right amount of salt and pepper make a wonderful seasoning, and a little ketchup and mustard can make just about anything worth eating. Barbecue sauce and salsa make a lot of cooks look real good, too, and neither is saved for a specific cuisine anymore.

But you shouldn't be satisfied with the basics of seasoning. There is a big wide world of flavors out there that takes ordinary food and makes it extraordinary. As cooks today, we have access to an amazing variety of spices and ingredients that our grandmothers never even dreamed of and I think we are remiss if we don't embrace these things and use them.

When I took a high school foods class in 1973, it was mostly focused on teaching girls how to cook for their families. It was all good food, but nothing we cooked was very interesting by today's standards. In suburban Chicago back then, tastes were still pretty simple for most people. At home, my grandmother Julia cooked dinner at our house most days. She had come to America from France as a child. She lived most of her life in a French community and, while she was a great cook, her recipes and techniques were very simple and very close to what she'd grown up with. We had meat, potatoes, veggies, and an occasional pasta dish just about every night. Her sauces were pan gravies. It was delicious, but relatively one-dimensional compared to what we eat today.

She never really knew anything about Mexican or Asian cuisine or the ingredients that are used to prepare those things. Korean bulgogi or jerk chicken weren't things she'd ever heard of; and while she probably would have loved it, she never even considered anything exotic like the Cocoa-Grilled Pork Tenderloin (page 128) or Flat-Iron Steak with Harissa (page 181) that you'll find in this book.

Things are different now, and we are lucky to have a wide variety of fun and interesting ingredients, tools, and techniques right at our fingertips. Yes, tools and techniques make great flavors, too. Grandma Julia knew how to season and cook food in her own simple way. She never thought of cooking food as a science, but I have. The science behind food and how it transforms—both in texture and flavor—when cooked is a fascinating subject. Learning even a little of it makes us much better cooks.

Brining is something Grandma might have used as a way to preserve things, but she never used it as a way to keep the pork chops from drying out when she cooked them. And she never even dreamt of injecting a flavored liquid into a piece of meat! Where would she have learned of such a thing or bought the injector if she did want to try it? She would have loved to have a high-quality instant-read thermometer, though, and it would have improved the consistency of her cooking, just like it does mine. But she never even imagined one with three-second speed. After all, she didn't have a local gourmet cookware store nearby. But I do, and I'm a better cook because of it.

All of these things together, with a little effort and attention to detail, can flavorize part of every meal you serve. In the chapters that follow, I'll be thorough about the different methods for soaking, poking, rubbing, and brushing your way to greatness.

All of these techniques will help, no matter what the cooking method, so please don't avoid a recipe because you don't like to use your broiler or you don't want to fire up the grill tonight. I always hope that you'll take my recipes and make them your own anyway. If you want to pan-fry one of my grilled recipes or grill one that I broiled, go for it! Use good methods for knowing when the food is done properly and you'll be fine. It's the same with ingredients. If you like things a little hotter, by all means fire it up! Like extra garlic? Go for it. Want to use bacon fat instead of butter? I love you! If you like a little less salt, just leave some out. But for brines, you'll need to keep all the salt in or it just won't work right. As you'll read in the Brines chapter, the salt level carries flavor and moisture into the meat, so if you lower the salt, that just won't happen. But like most things, eating a smaller portion might just be the solution to that problem.

The other method of soaking that we'll discuss here is marinating. This works just fine with a little less salt or just about any other adjustment, so feel free to customize to your heart's desire.

Injecting is really just a way to get a marinade deep into the meat, so anything goes there too; just remember that any particles that are bigger than your needle will have to be strained before using.

Rubbing and brushing are the tried-and-true methods of adding great flavors that we're all familiar with.

I hope that my recipes here will give you some new and fresh ideas and the inspiration to make your flavors just a little bit greater. Many of the marinade, injection, brine, rub, and glaze recipes in this book are very flexible and I hope you will use them in your own creative ways. For the sake of the cookbook, I've followed each with a recipe using them in a particular way, but please don't get stuck with only that idea! There are icons after each recipe that show you which meats or veggies I think will work best with those flavors. Use any of them and have fun doing it your way.

PROPERLY COOKED MEATS

These are the temps I recommend for properly cooking meat. All should be followed by resting the meat on a cutting board before slicing or serving it. I recommend a resting time of 3 minutes for steaks and chops, 5 to 10 minutes for medium-size pieces of meat, and 20 minutes for big roasts and birds.

Cooking Temperatures

Chicken breast	160°F (73°C)
Chicken legs, thighs, and wings	180°F (83°C)
Turkey breast	160°F (73°C)
Turkey legs, thighs, and wings	180°F (83°C)
Pork chops, tenderloins, and other lean cuts	150°F (65°C)
Pork shoulder for tender pulled pork	195°F (93°C)
Beef steaks and roasts (rare)	120°F (48°C)
Beef steaks and roasts (medium-rare)	125°F (50°C)
Ground beef	155°F (70°C)
Lamb chops and racks (medium-rare)	135°F (58°C)

WHAT I USE

These are the tools and ingredients that are in my kitchen. You won't find many gimmicky tools here. I use a couple of sharp knives and a cutting board for most jobs. I like these things and they work, so when I refer to an ingredient or a type of pan, grill, thermometer, etc., you'll know what I'm talking about.

Blender: I have a high-powered Vita-mix, and I think it's *the best*.

Broiler: The kind in a typical home oven with the pan set about 4 in (10 cm) below the heat.

Dutch Oven: A 6- to 8-qt (6- to 7.5-L) stainless-steel or enameled cast-iron pot.

Food Processor: I use a typical home food processor that can also be fitted with a smaller bowl that's great for grinding spices.

Injector: I use a low-priced kitchen injector and keep a couple spares around.

Instant-Read Thermometer: The best on the market is a Superfast Thermapen.

Knives: I use a very sharp 10-in (25-cm) chef knife and a 6-in (15-cm) boning knife for just about everything. My personal choice is the Shun Ken Onion line.

Large Skillet: A 12-in (30.5-cm) good-quality nonstick fry pan.

Medium Saucepan: A 2- to 3-qt (2- to 2.8-L) stainless-steel saucepan.

Outdoor Grill: A high-quality charcoal grill, with good temp control. (It's no secret that I prefer the Big Green Egg.)

Temperature Control Device for the Outdoor Grill: I use a BBQ Guru. The Digi-Q model is my preference.

MY FAVORITE INGREDIENTS

I use **Morton's Kosher Salt** for every recipe in this book. The brand is important because different brands have different-size granules, which can cause a discrepancy when measuring. Morton's Kosher weighs approximately 240 g per 1 cup. Not all salt weighs the same per cup, so if you are going to substitute, you will have to weigh your salt for the best results.

I use a medium-coarse **black pepper**, also known as restaurant-grind, unless otherwise specified.

Chili powder is one ingredient that I am a snob about. I buy San Antonio Red from Pendery's in Fort Worth, Texas. And as long as I'm ordering, I usually get my granulated onion, granulated garlic, and cumin from them, too, because the quality is top notch.

My **pork** comes from the supermarket or warehouse club.

When I refer to **beef**, it's USDA Choice graded, from the supermarket or warehouse club.

Chicken comes from the supermarket, but I try to avoid anything that has been enhanced with salt water or flavorings.

Turkey is bought frozen and thawed slowly in the refrigerator.

Seafood comes from a local fishmonger with a long record of selling good fresh fish.

Vegetables come from the freshest place I can find—a farmers' market when available, and the busiest supermarket when need be, to ensure good turnover.

MARINADES

Marinades are all about great flavor.

A marinade is a liquid that is highly seasoned and used to flavor and tenderize meats, seafood, and vegetables before cooking. It can be as simple as bottled Italian salad dressing or complex with a long list of exotic ingredients. Both work, and both have their place in the world of great flavor.

According to Harold McGee in *On Food and Cooking*, marinating meat goes back to the Renaissance era, when the primary function was to slow spoilage and provide flavor. You'll notice that almost all marinades contain an acidic base like vinegar, citrus juice, wine, or buttermilk. The acid helps to prevent meat deterioration, so historically this makes perfect sense. Acid also helps to tenderize meats, and that is a welcome side effect. The added flavor is always a bonus.

Today we all have refrigerators to slow spoilage, so we use marinades primarily to enhance flavor and to make things moist and tender. So all marinades usually also include oil to keep things juicy as well as salt, pepper, herbs, and spices to make it all taste good.

A marinade is sort of like brine, but it doesn't typically have a high salt content. That means it won't penetrate a protein as aggressively as a brine, which can be good or bad. The good news is that the food will be a little subtler in taste, particularly in saltiness, but the bad news is that it won't keep the meat as juicy if you overcook it. This is a common misunderstanding of the marinating process. I'm often asked what type of marinade I'd recommend for chicken breast to keep it from drying out. The truth is there is no such marinade. The solution is probably to quit overcooking that poor chicken breast. But what a marinade lacks in that regard is easily balanced by its ability to add great flavor to food by soaking it for an extended period of time and tenderize it with the acidic ingredients.

There is another kind of tenderizer that is often used in marinades—enzymatic ingredients such as pineapple or papaya. These fruits or their juices not only taste great but they contain papain, which is an excellent natural tenderizer. Avoid long soaking when using these, though, because the subject of the marinade can get over-tenderized and become soft and mushy.

If this all seems a little confusing, well, it is, but here is a simple rule to follow when choosing the meat that you want to marinate and deciding how long to soak it: The denser and thicker the cut of meat, the slower the process of marinating. So a big cut of a tough dense meat like a beef brisket just isn't going to work very well for marinating. But a 1-in (2.5-cm) thick pork chop is a great choice. Chicken and fish are not very dense, so they pick up the flavors of a marinade quickly.

But as with any rule like this, there are exceptions. A thick steak may only get a small amount of penetration from marinating, but if it's a bold-flavored marinade and a good-quality steak, a small amount may be all you need.

The recipes here are all fresh and meant to be used that way. A marinade can be made the night before and kept cold, but please don't make these days ahead and expect them to be as good as fresh. Once you have used a marinade on raw meat, it is never OK to reuse it. No matter how expensive the ingredients or how good it still looks, it is never OK to reuse a marinade. Don't serve it as a sauce either, unless you bring it to a full boil and cook it for 5 minutes. In most cases, I really wouldn't bother doing this. If you've marinated well and cook properly, you're not going to need that funky meat-juice sauce anyway.

This chapter begins with a basic and very simple marinade recipe. After that, the more elaborate recipes will have icons next to them suggesting which foods they are best suited for, followed by a complete recipe utilizing the marinade. With a little experimenting and some good ingredients, you're quickly going to learn to enjoy the powers of marinating.

THE BASIC MARINADE

Italian Dressing Marinade

This is a very simple marinade that's easy and much better than the stuff in the bottle. It's pretty good on a salad, too.

½ cup (120 ml) olive oil
½ cup (120 ml) vegetable oil
¼ cup (60 ml) red wine vinegar
4 garlic cloves, minced
1 tsp sugar
1 tsp dried oregano leaves
1 tsp dried basil leaves
1 tsp black pepper
½ tsp Morton's Kosher Salt

In a medium bowl, combine the olive oil, vegetable oil, vinegar, garlic, sugar, oregano, basil, pepper, and salt. Using a large whisk, mix the marinade vigorously until it is well blended. This may be made up to 12 hours ahead and kept covered in the refrigerator.

Makes about 1¼ cups (300 ml)

PINEAPPLE TERIYAKI MARINADE

This simple marinade combines the classic flavors of pineapple and teriyaki in a fresh and homemade way that beats bottled marinades every time.

½ cup (120 ml) soy sauce
½ cup (120 ml) pineapple juice
¼ cup (80 g) honey
4 garlic cloves, crushed
2 tbsp minced fresh ginger
1 tbsp sesame oil
½ tsp black pepper

In a medium bowl, combine the soy sauce, pineapple juice, honey, garlic, ginger, sesame oil, and pepper. Whisk until they are well blended. This may be made up to 12 hours ahead and kept covered in the refrigerator.

Makes about 1½ cups (360 ml)

Pineapple Teriyaki Pork Chops

These grilled pork chops really stand out with their great island flavor. You could easily substitute pork blade steaks here for an interesting change of pace. I'd serve white rice and fresh grilled pineapple slices with this.

> 4 boneless pork chops, about ¾ in (2 cm) thick
> 1 recipe Pineapple Teriyaki Marinade (page 19)

Place the chops in a large heavy-duty zip-top bag. Pour the marinade over the chops. Seal the bag, squeezing out as much air as possible. Move the chops around so they are well coated with the marinade. Refrigerate them for 4 to 6 hours, occasionally moving the chops around within the bag to make sure they remain well coated.

Prepare an outdoor grill to cook direct over medium heat. Take the chops from the marinade, shaking off any excess, and place them on the grill. Discard any remaining marinade. Cook them for 10 to 12 minutes, turning them often, until the chops are golden brown and reach an internal temperature of 150°F (65°C) in the thickest part of the meat. Transfer the chops to a plate. Tent them loosely with foil and let them rest for 5 minutes, then serve one chop to each guest.

Makes 4 servings

CHINESE CHAR SIU MARINADE

Char siu is a Cantonese barbecue marinade. It's a little sweet and a little sticky and packed with great flavor. If you want it very red like some restaurants do it, just add a little bit of red food coloring.

¼ cup (60 ml) hoisin sauce
¼ cup (80 g) honey
2 tbsp soy sauce
1 tbsp mirin
½ tsp Morton's Kosher Salt
½ tsp white pepper
½ tsp granulated garlic
½ tsp five-spice powder

In a medium bowl, combine the hoisin, honey, soy sauce, mirin, salt, pepper, granulated garlic, and five-spice powder. Whisk until they are well blended. This may be made up to 12 hours ahead and kept covered in the refrigerator.

Makes about ¾ cup (180 ml)

Char Siu Pork Loin

This is the tasty red barbecue pork that you get at the Chinese restaurant. It's good fresh and thinly sliced as an appetizer or added to just about any rice dish you can dream up for dinner.

2 lb (910 g) boneless pork loin in one piece
1 recipe Chinese Char Siu Marinade (facing page)

Cut the loin into strips about 1½ in (4 cm) square. Place them in a large heavy-duty zip-top bag. Pour the marinade over the pork. Seal the bag, squeezing out as much air as possible. Move the pork strips around in the bag so they are well coated with the marinade. Refrigerate them for 24 hours, occasionally moving the pork around within the bag to make sure it remains well coated.

Prepare an outdoor grill to cook indirect at 350°F (175°C). Take the pork from the marinade, shaking off any excess, and place it on the grill. Pour the marinade into a saucepan and bring it to a boil for 5 minutes. After the pork has been cooking for 15 minutes, baste it with the boiled marinade and then flip over the pieces. Baste them again and cook them for another 15 minutes, until the pork reaches an internal temperature of 150°F (65°C). Baste it one last time and then transfer the pork to a plate. Discard the remaining marinade. Tent the pork loosely with foil and let it rest for 5 minutes. Slice it thinly to serve.

Makes about 8 servings

CUBAN MOJO MARINADE

Homemade mojo is the true flavor of Miami and it's delicious. Real sour orange juice is key to a good mojo. If you can't find it at your store, you can order it online or use the substitute below.

2 cups (480 ml) sour orange juice (or 1½ cups [360 ml] orange juice and ½ cup [120 ml] lime juice)

¼ cup (60 ml) olive oil

10 garlic cloves, crushed

6 scallions, white and green parts coarsely chopped

2 large chipotle chiles in adobo sauce, coarsely chopped

2 tbsp Morton's Kosher Salt

1 tbsp black pepper

2 tsp ground cumin

2 tsp dried oregano leaves

In the pitcher of a blender, combine the sour orange juice, olive oil, garlic, scallions, chipotles, salt, pepper, cumin, and oregano. Blend them on high speed for about 1 minute, until all the big chunks are gone. Pour the mojo into a nonreactive bowl and refrigerate it until ready to use. This may be made up to 12 hours ahead and kept covered in the refrigerator.

Makes about 2½ cups (600 ml)

Mojo Country Ribs

Country ribs are a great way to bring the mojo to the grill. Pull the meat from the bones if you want to try a Cuban sandwich, or just serve the ribs next to the classic Cuban sides of black beans and white rice.

> 3 lb (1.5 kg) country-style ribs, cut from the loin
> 1 recipe Cuban Mojo Marinade (page 24)
> 1 small onion, thinly sliced

Place the ribs in a large heavy-duty zip-top bag. Pour the marinade over the ribs. Seal the bag, squeezing out as much air as possible. Move the ribs around within the bag so they are well coated with the marinade. Refrigerate them for 8 to 10 hours, occasionally moving the ribs around within the bag to make sure they remain well coated.

Prepare an outdoor grill to cook direct over medium-high heat. Take the ribs from the marinade, shaking off any excess, and place them on the grill. Discard any remaining marinade. Cook the ribs for 5 to 6 minutes, until they're golden brown, then flip them over. Cook them for another 5 to 6 minutes, until the ribs reach an internal temperature of 150°F (65°C) in the thickest part of the meat. Country ribs may be different sizes, so you may have to remove the finished smaller pieces while continuing to cook the larger ones. As they finish, transfer the ribs to a platter and, when they are all on the plate, tent them loosely with foil. Let the ribs rest for 5 minutes. Top the ribs with the raw onion and serve them family style.

Makes 4 servings

CHARDONNAY MARINADE

White wine always makes a great marinade as long as you remember the golden rule: Don't ever cook with a wine that you wouldn't drink.

> ¾ cup (180 ml) Chardonnay
> ¼ cup (60 ml) olive oil
> Juice of ½ lemon
> 1 tsp Morton's Kosher Salt
> 1 tsp black pepper
> 1 tsp dried thyme leaves
> ½ tsp granulated garlic
> ½ tsp granulated onion

In a medium bowl, combine the Chardonnay, olive oil, lemon juice, salt, pepper, thyme, granulated garlic, and granulated onion. Whisk until they are well blended. This may be made up to 12 hours ahead and kept covered in the refrigerator.

Makes about 1 cup (240 ml)

Chardonnay Chicken Breast

I like to serve this fresh-tasting chicken on top of a romaine salad with lemon wedges to squeeze over the top as a great luncheon dish or a light summer dinner.

> 4 boneless skinless chicken breasts, about 2 lb (910 g) total
> 1 recipe Chardonnay Marinade (page 27)
> 1 tbsp chopped fresh parsley

Place the chicken breasts on a cutting board and pound them gently with a meat mallet just until they are an even thickness. Place the breasts in a large heavy-duty zip-top bag. Pour the marinade over them. Seal the bag, squeezing out as much air as possible. Move the breasts around within the bag so they are well coated with the marinade. Refrigerate them for 4 to 6 hours, occasionally moving the breasts around in the bag to make sure they remain well coated.

Prepare an outdoor grill to cook direct over medium-high heat. Take the breasts from the marinade, shaking off any excess, and place them on the grill. Discard any remaining marinade. Cook the chicken for 6 to 7 minutes, until it is golden brown on the bottom. Flip the breasts over and cook them for another 6 to 7 minutes, until they're golden brown and reach an internal temperature of 160°F (73°C). Transfer them to a plate and tent them loosely with foil. Let the chicken rest for 5 minutes. Sprinkle it with the parsley to serve.

Makes 4 servings

JALAPEÑO-BUTTERMILK MARINADE

The enzymes in buttermilk act as a natural tenderizer and the jalapeño provides a nice fresh kick of flavor in this marinade. It's a perfect start for fried chicken, but also works well for grilled foods.

2 tbsp olive oil

1 small yellow onion, chopped

4 jalapeños, seeded and chopped

2 garlic cloves, chopped

2 cups (480 ml) buttermilk

2 tsp Morton's Kosher Salt

1 tsp black pepper

Heat the olive oil in a medium skillet over medium-low heat. Add the onion, jalapeños, and garlic and cook them, stirring often until they are soft, 7 to 8 minutes. Transfer the vegetables to a plate to cool.

In the pitcher of a blender, combine the buttermilk, salt, pepper, and jalapeño mixture. Blend them on high speed for 30 seconds, until they are well combined. This may be made up to 12 hours ahead and kept covered in the refrigerator.

Makes about 2½ cups (600 ml)

Jalapeño Fried Chicken Breast

Buttermilk marinade is the secret to fried chicken that's tender and juicy. I've suggested boneless breasts here, but don't hesitate to use any boneless or bone-in chicken parts. At my house, fried chicken always gets served with mashed potatoes and gravy.

4 boneless skinless chicken breasts, about 2 lb (910 g) total
1 recipe Jalapeño-Buttermilk Marinade (facing page)
¾ cup (90 g) all-purpose flour
¼ cup (30 g) dry bread crumbs
2 tbsp cornstarch
2 tsp Morton's Kosher Salt
½ tsp black pepper
½ tsp granulated garlic
½ tsp granulated onion
Vegetable oil for frying

Place the chicken breasts on a cutting board and pound them gently with a meat mallet just until they are an even thickness. Place the breasts in a large heavy-duty zip-top bag. Pour the marinade over them. Seal the bag, squeezing out as much air as possible. Move the breasts around within the bag so they are well coated with the marinade. Refrigerate them for 4 to 6 hours, occasionally moving the breasts around in the bag to make sure they remain well coated.

On a large flat plate, combine the flour, bread crumbs, cornstarch, salt, pepper, granulated garlic, and granulated onion. Remove the breasts one at a time from the marinade, shaking off any excess. Dredge the breasts in the flour mixture, coating them well on all sides. Lay each breast on a wire rack set over a baking sheet to rest. Let them rest for 15 minutes.

Add enough vegetable oil to a large skillet to reach a depth of ½ in (12 mm). Heat the oil over medium-high heat to a temperature of 325°F (165°C). Two at a time, add the chicken to the hot oil. Cook the chicken for 6 to 7 minutes, until it is golden brown on the bottom. Flip the breasts over and cook them for another 6 to 7 minutes, until they're golden brown and reach an internal temperature of 160°F (73°C). Transfer them to a clean wire rack to rest for 5 minutes before serving. Serve the chicken family-style, allowing for one whole breast per person.

Makes 4 servings

TRADITIONAL TANDOORI MARINADE

Tandoori is the classic Indian marinade made with yogurt and strong curry spices like cumin, coriander, and garam masala, which produce a unique and tasty flavor.

2 cups (480 ml) plain yogurt
2 tbsp minced fresh ginger
8 garlic cloves, crushed
Juice of 1 lime
1½ tbsp Morton's Kosher Salt
1 tbsp ground cumin
1 tbsp garam masala
1 tsp paprika
1 tsp ground coriander
1 tsp turmeric
1 tsp chili powder
½ tsp cayenne

In a medium bowl, combine the yogurt, ginger, garlic, lime juice, salt, cumin, garam masala, paprika, ground coriander, turmeric, chili powder, and cayenne. Whisk until they are well blended. This may be made up to 12 hours ahead and kept covered in the refrigerator.

Makes about 2 cups (480 ml)

Tandoori Chicken Legs

The traditional tandoor cooking method involves a clay vessel and a wood fire, but the outdoor grill that most of us have at home does a respectable job. Just keep it hot and don't be afraid to get the edges of the chicken a little browned. These go well with pita wedges and a fresh green salad.

8 large skinless chicken drumsticks, about 1½ lb (700 g) total
1 recipe Traditional Tandoori Marinade (facing page)

With a sharp knife, cut a deep slash on an angle into the meat on each side of the drumsticks. Place them in a large heavy-duty zip-top bag. Pour the marinade over them. Seal the bag, squeezing out as much air as possible. Move the drumsticks around within the bag so they are well coated with the marinade. Refrigerate them for 4 to 6 hours, occasionally moving the drumsticks around in the bag to make sure they remain well coated.

Prepare an outdoor grill to cook direct over medium-high heat. Take the drumsticks from the marinade, shaking off any excess, and place them on the grill. Discard any remaining marinade. Cook them for 30 to 40 minutes, turning the drumsticks often until the chicken is golden brown with a few crunchy edges and reaches an internal temperature of 180°F (83°C). Transfer the drumsticks to a plate and tent them loosely with foil. Let them rest for 5 minutes. Serve two pieces to each guest.

Makes 4 servings

SOUTHWESTERN MARINADE

This is a sweet and fresh-tasting marinade with great balance. Add another serrano or two if you want to heat it up.

> ¼ cup (60 ml) olive oil
> Juice of 2 limes
> 2 Roma tomatoes, coarsely chopped
> 6 scallions, white and green parts coarsely chopped
> ½ cup (15 g) chopped fresh cilantro
> 2 serrano chiles, chopped
> ¼ cup (60 ml) agave nectar
> 3 garlic cloves, crushed
> 1 tbsp chili powder
> 1½ tsp Morton's Kosher Salt
> ½ tsp black pepper

In the pitcher of a blender, combine the olive oil, lime juice, tomatoes, scallions, cilantro, chiles, agave nectar, garlic, chili powder, salt, and pepper. Blend them on high speed for about 1 minute, until everything is well pureed. This may be made up to 12 hours ahead and kept covered in the refrigerator.

Makes about 1 cup (240 ml)

Southwestern Chicken Thighs

These tangy and spicy chicken thighs are great party food served up with refried beans, yellow rice, salsa, and warm corn tortillas.

8 boneless skinless chicken thighs, about 3 lb (1.6 kg) total
1 recipe Southwestern Marinade (facing page)

The night before you plan to cook, put the thighs in a large heavy-duty zip-top bag. Pour the marinade over the thighs, coating them well. Seal the bag, squeezing out as much air as possible. Move the thighs around within the bag so they are well coated with the marinade. Refrigerate them for at least 8 hours, and up to 24, occasionally massaging the meat to make sure it remains well coated.

Prepare an outdoor grill to cook direct over medium-high heat. Take the thighs from the marinade, shaking off any excess, and place them on the grill. Discard any remaining marinade. Cook them for 3 to 4 minutes per side, until the bottoms of the thighs are golden brown. Flip them over and cook them for another 3 to 4 minutes, until the second side is golden brown and the thighs reach an internal temperature of 180°F (83°C). Remove the chicken to a plate and serve two thighs to each guest.

Makes 4 servings

KOREAN BULGOGI MARINADE

Bulgogi is a Korean flavor combination similar to the more familiar teriyaki, with a bit more of a refined flavor from the addition of sesame seeds and pear. If you want it hot, just add more red chili flakes.

- ¼ cup (35 g) sesame seeds
- 1 cup (240 ml) soy sauce
- 15 scallions, white and green parts sliced thinly on the bias
- ¼ cup (50 g) sugar
- 6 garlic cloves, crushed
- ¼ cup (60 ml) sesame oil
- ½ ripe pear, grated
- 2 tbsp honey
- 1 tsp red chili flakes

In a medium skillet over low heat, toast the sesame seeds, tossing them often, for 1 to 2 minutes, just until you begin to smell them toasting. Remove them to a small plate to cool.

In a medium bowl, combine the soy sauce, scallions, sugar, garlic, sesame oil, pear, honey, chili flakes, and toasted sesame seeds. Whisk until they are well blended. This may be made up to 12 hours ahead and kept covered in the refrigerator.

Makes about 2 cups (480 ml)

Bulgogi Short Ribs

The great flavor of short ribs with bold bulgogi sauce is a legendary combination, and the cross-cut style marinates and cooks quickly. Perfect with rice and mixed greens.

> 4 lb (1.8 kg) USDA Choice beef short ribs cut crosswise, about ½ in (12 mm) thick
> 1 recipe Korean Bulgogi Marinade (page 38)
> 2 scallions, white and green parts sliced thinly on the bias

Place the ribs in a large baking dish, overlapping them as needed. Pour the marinade over the ribs. Move the ribs around so they are well coated with the marinade. Cover and refrigerate them for 1 hour. Remove the dish and flip the ribs over, coating them well in the marinade. Cover and refrigerate them for 1 hour more. Remove the dish and flip the ribs again, coating them well with the marinade. Cover and let the ribs rest for 1 hour at room temperature.

Prepare an outdoor grill to cook indirect over medium heat. Flip the ribs over again in the marinade, coating them well. Cover the pan with aluminum foil and cook the ribs for 90 minutes. Transfer the ribs to a plate. Remove as much fat as possible from the pan liquid.

Prepare the grill to cook direct over medium heat. Transfer the ribs to the grill and cook them, turning often and basting them with the pan liquid, until they are golden brown on both sides, about 15 minutes. Transfer the ribs to a plate and tent them loosely with foil. Let them rest for 5 minutes. Transfer them to a platter and top with the scallions to serve them family-style.

Makes 4 servings

COKE SOAK

This is a tasty marinade for meat, with a sweet background and familiar flavors in an unexpected combination.

1 cup (240 ml) Coca-Cola
½ cup (120 ml) soy sauce
¼ cup (60 ml) Worcestershire sauce
¼ cup (80 g) honey
1 tbsp granulated garlic
1 tbsp granulated onion
1 tbsp good-quality chili powder
1 tsp Morton's Kosher Salt
1 tsp black pepper
½ tsp cayenne

In a medium bowl, combine the Coke, soy sauce, Worcestershire, honey, granulated garlic, granulated onion, chili powder, salt, pepper, and cayenne. Whisk until they are well blended. This may be made up to 12 hours ahead and kept covered in the refrigerator.

Makes about 2 cups (480 ml)

Coke-Soaked Rib-Eyes

Rib-eye steak gets a nice fresh update with the classic flavor of Coke mixed with a few savory friends. All you need next to these is a baked potato and grilled corn on the cob.

4 USDA Choice rib-eye steaks, about 1 in (2.5 cm) thick
1 recipe Coke Soak (facing page)

Place the steaks in a large heavy-duty zip-top bag. Pour the marinade over the steaks. Seal the bag, squeezing out as much air as possible. Move the steaks around within the bag so they are well coated with the marinade. Refrigerate them for 4 to 6 hours, occasionally moving the steaks around within the bag to make sure they remain well coated.

Prepare an outdoor grill to cook direct over medium-high heat. Take the steaks from the marinade and pat them dry with a paper towel. Discard any remaining marinade. Place them on the grill. Cook the steaks for 5 to 6 minutes, until they're golden brown, then flip them over. Cook them for another 5 to 6 minutes, until the steaks reach an internal temperature of 125°F (50°C) in the thickest part of the meat for medium-rare. Transfer the steaks to a plate and tent them loosely with aluminum foil. Let them rest for 5 minutes. Serve one steak to each guest.

Makes 4 servings

FRESH PAPAYA MARINADE

Fresh papaya contains papain, a natural tenderizer with great flavor. Don't marinate the meat for too long, though, or it will get mushy. Four hours for pork or poultry and 8 hours for beef is the max.

> 2 cups (320 g) 1-in (2.5-cm) cubed ripe papaya
> ½ cup (120 ml) soy sauce
> 2 tbsp olive oil
> 2 tbsp honey
> 3 garlic cloves, crushed
> 1 tsp chili powder
> 1 tsp black pepper

Place the papaya, soy sauce, olive oil, honey, garlic, chili powder, and pepper in a medium bowl. With a potato masher, smash the papaya until it's well blended with the other ingredients. This may be made up to 12 hours ahead and kept covered in the refrigerator.

Makes about 1½ cups (360 ml)

Papaya-Grilled Flank Steak

Pay attention to the marinade time for this recipe, as the papaya is a powerful tenderizer. Flank steaks are always best served rare to medium-rare and sliced thinly against the grain. This goes well with fried rice and a green vegetable.

2 lb (910 g) flank steak
1 recipe Fresh Papaya Marinade (facing page)
Morton's Kosher Salt
Black pepper

With a sharp knife, cut very shallow slashes in the steak on a 45-degree angle to the grain, about 1 in (2.5 cm) apart. Repeat the process in the opposite direction to form a cross-hatch pattern. Flip the steak over and repeat the cross-hatching on the second side. Place the steak in a large heavy-duty zip-top bag. Pour the marinade over the steak. Seal the bag, squeezing out as much air as possible. Move the steak around within the bag so it is well coated with the marinade. Refrigerate it for about 8 hours, occasionally moving the steak around within the bag to make sure it remains well coated.

Prepare an outdoor grill to cook direct over high heat. Take the steak from the marinade and pat it dry with a paper towel. Discard any remaining marinade. Season the steak lightly with salt and pepper. Place it on the grill and cook the steak for 4 to 5 minutes, until it is golden brown. Flip the steak over and cook it for another 4 to 5 minutes, until it's golden brown and reaches an internal temperature of 120°F (48°C) for rare. Transfer the steak to a plate and tent it loosely with foil. Let it rest for 5 minutes. With a sharp knife, slice the steak thinly against the grain. Arrange the slices evenly on a platter to serve.

Makes 4 servings

POULTRY   FISH   VEGGIES   FRUIT

BIG BAD STEAK MARINADE

Just as it's named, this marinade is bold and not for any wimpy meats or wimpy palates.

 1 cup (240 ml) full-bodied red wine
 ½ cup (120 ml) olive oil
 ½ cup (120 ml) fresh orange juice
 ¼ cup (60 ml) soy sauce
 12 garlic cloves, coarsely chopped
 4 sprigs fresh rosemary, stripped from the stem
 2 tsp black pepper
 1 tsp Morton's Kosher Salt

In the pitcher of a blender, combine the wine, olive oil, orange juice, soy sauce, garlic, rosemary, pepper, and salt. Blend them on high speed for about 30 seconds until they are mixed well. This may be made up to 12 hours ahead and kept covered in the refrigerator.

 Makes about 2¼ cups (540 ml)

Big Bad New York Strip Steaks

This recipe takes your steaks to another level of flavor when you want something just a little bolder. Serve them with homemade french fries and a wedge salad.

4 USDA Choice New York strip steaks, about 1½ in (4 cm) thick
1 recipe Big Bad Steak Marinade (page 46)
Morton's Kosher Salt
Black pepper

Place the steaks in a large heavy-duty zip-top bag. Pour the marinade over the steaks. Seal the bag, squeezing out as much air as possible. Move the steaks around within the bag so they are well coated with the marinade. Refrigerate them for about 10 hours, occasionally moving the steaks around within the bag to make sure they remain well coated.

Prepare an outdoor grill to cook direct over medium-high heat. Take the steaks from the marinade and pat them dry with a paper towel. Discard any remaining marinade. Season them on both sides with salt and pepper. Place the steaks on the grill and cook them for 4 to 5 minutes, until they are well browned. Flip the steaks over and cook them for another 4 to 5 minutes, until they're well browned on the second side and reach an internal temperature of 125°F (50°C) for medium-rare. Remove the steaks to a platter and tent them loosely with aluminum foil. Let them rest for 5 minutes. Serve one steak to each guest.

Makes 4 servings

MEDITERRANEAN MARINADE

The tangy flavors of the lemon, garlic, and herbs enhance any grilled meats, but lamb is by far the most popular choice. If you use this with fish, just a quick 30-minute soak will do.

½ cup (120 ml) olive oil
Juice of 1 lemon
8 garlic cloves, crushed
1 tbsp Morton's Kosher Salt
1 tsp dried oregano
½ tsp black pepper
½ tsp dried thyme
½ tsp Sugar In The Raw or other raw sugar

In a medium bowl, combine the olive oil, lemon juice, garlic, salt, oregano, pepper, thyme, and raw sugar. Whisk until they are well blended. This may be made up to 12 hours ahead and kept covered in the refrigerator.

Makes about ¾ cup (180 ml)

Mediterranean Grilled Lamb Chops

Lamb chops are quickly flavored with this marinade, but you could substitute racks of lamb or even a butterflied leg with great results. Oven-roasted potatoes and veggies would pair perfectly with this dish.

8 lamb loin chops, about 1¼ in (3.5 cm) thick
1 recipe Mediterranean Marinade (page 49)

Place the chops in a large heavy-duty zip-top bag. Pour the marinade over the chops. Seal the bag, squeezing out as much air as possible. Move the chops around within the bag so they are well coated with the marinade. Refrigerate them for 4 to 12 hours, occasionally moving the chops around within the bag to make sure they remain well coated.

Prepare an outdoor grill to cook indirect over medium heat. Take the chops from the marinade, shaking off any excess. Discard any remaining marinade. Place them on the grill and cook them for 5 to 6 minutes, until they are golden brown on the bottom. Flip the chops over and cook them for another 5 to 6 minutes, until they're golden brown on the bottom and reach an internal temperature of 135°F (55°C) for medium-rare. Transfer the chops to a plate and tent them loosely with foil. Let them rest for 5 minutes. Serve two chops to each diner.

Makes 4 servings

BOURBON STREET MARINADE

This marinade is a tip of the hat to the classic New Orleans barbecued shrimp dish. It makes a pretty good dipping sauce for crusty bread too.

>   ¼ cup (60 ml) olive oil
>   Juice of 1 lemon
>   2 tbsp Louisiana hot sauce
>   2 tbsp Worcestershire sauce
>   2 tbsp bourbon
>   1 tbsp honey
>   1 tbsp soy sauce
>   ½ tsp black pepper
>   ½ tsp granulated garlic
>   ½ tsp granulated onion
>   ¼ tsp ground thyme
>   ¼ tsp cayenne, or more to taste

In a medium bowl, combine the olive oil, lemon juice, hot sauce, Worcestershire, bourbon, honey, soy sauce, pepper, granulated garlic, granulated onion, thyme, and cayenne. Whisk until they are well blended. This may be made up to 12 hours ahead and kept covered in the refrigerator.

Makes about ¾ cup (180 ml)

New Orleans–Style Spicy Grilled Shrimp

In the spirit of sustainable eating and great flavor, I always prefer wild American Gulf shrimp for this recipe, and the bigger the better. White rice and crusty bread are what you should serve alongside.

1 lb (455 g) jumbo shrimp, peeled and deveined
1 recipe Bourbon Street Marinade (page 51)

Place the shrimp in a large heavy-duty zip-top bag. Pour the marinade over the shrimp. Seal the bag, squeezing out as much air as possible. Move the shrimp around within the bag so they are well coated with the marinade. Refrigerate them for about 4 hours, occasionally moving the shrimp around within the bag to make sure they remain well coated. Soak eight bamboo skewers in water for 1 hour before you plan to cook.

Prepare an outdoor grill to cook direct over medium-high heat. Take the shrimp from the marinade and lay them flat on a cutting board. Line them up in four lines. Slide a skewer through the shrimp in each line. Then slide a second skewer into each line parallel to the first. Drizzle 1 to 2 Tbsp of the marinade over each shrimp skewer and then discard the remainder. Place the shrimp on the grill. Cook them for 4 to 5 minutes, until they are lightly browned and opaque on the bottom. Flip them over and cook them for another 4 to 5 minutes, until they are golden brown and opaque on the bottom and firm to the touch. Remove the shrimp to a platter to serve.

Makes 2 servings

SESAME-GINGER MARINADE

Inspired by a dish I created for a dinner with the Graham Rahal Indy Car Race Team, this recipe is a tasty and fun marinade that easily doubles as a salad dressing.

> ½ cup (120 ml) sesame oil
> ⅓ cup (80 ml) agave nectar
> ¼ cup (60 ml) olive oil
> ¼ cup (25 g) finely minced fresh ginger
> ¼ cup (60 ml) rice vinegar
> 2 tbsp fish sauce
> 2 tbsp soy sauce
> Juice of ½ lime
> 4 garlic cloves, crushed
> 1 tsp Morton's Kosher Salt
> ½ tsp white pepper

In a medium bowl, combine the sesame oil, agave nectar, olive oil, ginger, vinegar, fish sauce, soy sauce, lime juice, garlic, salt, and pepper. Whisk vigorously until they are well blended. This may be made up to 12 hours ahead and kept covered in the refrigerator.

Makes about 1 cup (240 ml)

Mixed Veggie Grill

Veggies on the grill are a great addition to any barbecue party, and these might even steal the show. Serve them next to just about anything.

2 medium yellow squash

2 medium zucchini

1 recipe Sesame-Ginger Marinade (page 53)

1 large red bell pepper

2 thick slices red onion

3 garlic cloves, crushed

1 tbsp minced fresh tarragon

Morton's Kosher Salt

1 tsp black pepper

¼ cup (30 g) shaved Parmesan cheese

Split the squash and zucchini lengthwise and place them in a large heavy-duty zip-top bag. Add three-fourths of the marinade and seal the bag, squeezing out as much air as possible. Move the veggies around within the bag so they are well coated with the marinade. Refrigerate them for at least 2 hours, and up to 8, occasionally moving the veggies around within the bag to make sure they remain well coated.

Prepare an outdoor grill to cook direct over medium-high heat. Grill the bell pepper until charred on all sides. Place in a small paper bag and set it aside to rest. Take the squash and zucchini from the marinade and place them on the grill cut-side down. Reserve the marinade. Add the slices of onion to the grill. Cook everything for 3 to 4 minutes, until it is golden brown on the bottom. Flip over the squash, zucchini, and onion and cook them for another 3 to 4 minutes, until they are golden brown on the bottom and just tender. Remove everything to a cutting board. As soon as it's cool enough to handle, cut the squash and zucchini into bite-size pieces. Chop the onion. Peel the charred skin from the bell pepper. Core, seed, and cut it into 1-by-¼-in (2.5-cm-by-6-mm) strips.

In a large bowl, combine the squash, zucchini, onion, bell pepper, garlic, tarragon, 1 tsp salt, pepper, and the reserved marinade. Toss it all well to mix. Taste for salt and add more if necessary. Transfer the mixture to a shallow serving bowl and top it with the Parmesan before serving.

Makes about 6 servings

BALSAMIC AND GARLIC MARINADE

This is a marinade with big flavor and a little twang. No need to use the high-price balsamic here, though. Add some extra garlic if you're in the mood.

⅓ cup (80 ml) balsamic vinegar
⅓ cup (80 ml) olive oil
5 garlic cloves, crushed
1 tsp Morton's Kosher Salt
½ tsp dried thyme
½ tsp dried marjoram
½ tsp black pepper

In the pitcher of a blender, combine the balsamic, olive oil, garlic, salt, thyme, marjoram, and pepper. Blend them on high speed for about 20 seconds, until smooth. This may be made up to 12 hours ahead and kept covered in the refrigerator.

Makes about ⅔ cup (160 ml)

Grilled Portobellos

These are great as an appetizer for two, served hot and whole or cut into squares and served with toothpicks as a canapé at room temp. If you're feeding more, just double or triple the recipe as needed.

2 large portobello mushrooms
1 recipe Balsamic and Garlic Marinade (page 57)
¼ cup (30 g) shredded Parmesan cheese

Remove the stems and place the portobellos in a large heavy-duty zip-top bag. Pour the marinade over the portobellos. Seal the bag, squeezing out as much air as possible. Move the portobellos around within the bag so they are well coated with the marinade. Refrigerate them for 2 to 4 hours, occasionally moving them around within the bag to make sure they remain well coated.

Prepare an outdoor grill to cook direct over medium-high heat. Take the portobellos from the marinade and place them on the grill gill-side down. Discard any remaining marinade. Cook them for 4 to 5 minutes, until the bottoms begin to brown and soften. Flip the portobellos over and top each with half of the cheese. Cook them for another 4 to 5 minutes, until the portobellos are al dente and the cheese is hot and bubbly. Using a large spatula, transfer them to individual plates to serve.

Makes 2 servings

INJECTIONS

The art of injecting food is a fairly recent trend for the home cook, but it works well and it's a fun way to bring great flavor deep inside of large cuts of meat before cooking.

We've all tried to marinate or dry-rub a big piece of meat and been disappointed to learn that the flavors just didn't penetrate as deeply as we'd hoped, leaving the inside meat bland. Brining works better for this, but we don't always want the salty aspect to our flavors.

The solution to the dilemma is to inject a flavored liquid deeply into the meat before cooking. This process has been used for years in big commercial food applications. Once the injected food is cooked and sliced, the inside meat tastes well seasoned and the texture is juicy and luscious. It's a beautiful thing to see the layers of liquid-flavor goodness dripping from the inside as an injected roast or turkey is sliced.

I remember the first time I saw this process on TV, when a guy from Louisiana injected and then deep-fried a turkey. It looked so good! I also remember thinking that I just had to get in on this. So I went to the farm store and bought a big syringe intended for giving a medicinal shot to livestock. I filled it with melted butter and sherry and injected a turkey before smoking it. It was so good that it inspired me to enter it in the 1991 Illinois State Barbecue Championships, where I won my first-ever cooking trophy. I have won a few hundred since then, but that trophy is still in my office. I still use that recipe, too, and it's just as good—but these days, I buy my syringes from the grocery or cooking store. Injecting the meat at a barbecue competition wasn't done much back then, but these days all the top cooks do it. They inject whole hogs, big briskets, and pork butts to add flavor and moisture deep inside those big cuts. Some cooks even inject their ribs with a small dose in-between the bones.

But what are they using to flavor these things? The practice really picked up steam when the guys who cook whole hogs began making a concoction of apple juice, sugar, vinegar, hot sauce, and some barbecue rub. This process quickly spread to the teams cooking pork butts and whole pork shoulders, and eventually the brisket cooks joined in. But then along came Joe Ames, with his Fab-B concoction designed specifically for beef, and for sale to anyone who wanted it. Fab-B included phosphates to help keep the brisket moist and juicy while adding great flavor. Once again, this was a commercial process brought to the home cook and it changed the world of competition barbecue forever.

These days, there are many versions of this brisket injection available, and nearly all of the top competition cooks are using one of them. Just search online for "competition brisket injection," and you'll find a recipe.

For typical home cooks, making an injection is pretty simple: You start with a liquid or combination of liquids and add some spices. Just about any marinade recipe can be converted to an injection liquid, too. The only real rule is that it must be strained. Garlic chunks or even large spices will clog the injector needle. I find it easier to use high-quality ground spices instead of fresh garlic or onion, which have to be strained out. You'll also need to be aware of the salt content of a marinade recipe, because unlike a marinade, the injection liquid will all stay with the meat. Either use less salt or don't inject too much of the liquid. Last, but not least, for safety's sake always discard any unused injection liquid immediately. It'll be contaminated by the needle going back and forth and not suitable for anything else.

Some of the injection recipes here may call for more than you'll need. A good solution is to divide the batch before dipping the needle in, then reserve a clean portion for later use. These recipes can be refrigerated safely for up to a week.

This chapter begins with a basic and very simple injection recipe. After that, the more elaborate recipes will have icons next to them suggesting which foods they are best suited for, followed by a complete recipe utilizing the injection. Now go get a syringe and start injecting things! The great flavors will make you and your guests very happy.

THE BASIC INJECTION

Fast Flavor Injection

This simple injection will brighten up the taste of just about anything from the inside out. Feel free to substitute half of the water with a mild fruit juice, white wine, or beer.

1 cup (240 ml) water
1 tbsp sugar
1 tbsp soy sauce
1 tbsp Louisiana hot sauce
1 tsp Morton's Kosher Salt

In a small bowl, combine the water, sugar, soy sauce, hot sauce, and salt. With a fork or a whisk, mix everything until well blended. Cover and refrigerate the mixture for up to 1 week.

Makes about 1 cup (240 ml)

SECRET APPLE JUICE INJECTION

Apple juice is great place to start when making a pork injection and is the secret to many of the great recipes used by barbecue contest champions. Once apple juice and pork are in the mix, the other combinations are endless, so feel free to customize this one with your favorite flavors.

1½ cups (360 ml) apple juice
¼ cup (50 g) Sugar In The Raw or other raw sugar
1 tbsp Morton's Kosher Salt
2 tbsp yellow mustard
2 tbsp soy sauce
½ tsp cayenne

In a medium bowl, combine the apple juice, raw sugar, salt, mustard, soy sauce, and cayenne. With a fork or whisk, mix everything until well blended. Cover and refrigerate the mixture for up to 1 week.

Makes about 2 cups (480 ml)

Spare Rib Surprise

The surprise here is all of the flavor next to the bone from the flavorful injection. Macaroni and cheese and collard greens will go very well on this table.

> 2 slabs (about 4 lb [1.8 kg] each) whole spareribs
> 1 recipe Secret Apple Juice Injection (facing page)
> 1 cup (220 g) barbecue rub such as Barbecue Rub #34 (page 133)
> ½ cup (120 ml) apple juice

A half hour before you plan to cook, peel the membrane off the back of the ribs and cut the flap of meat across the bone side off. Trim any excess fat.

Using a kitchen injector, inject the ribs in between the bones from both ends until all of the injection liquid has been used up. Season the ribs liberally on both sides with the rub. Refrigerate them until needed.

Prepare a barbecue pit or outdoor grill to cook indirect at 275°F (135°C) using a small amount of applewood for flavor. Place the ribs meaty-side up on the grill and close the lid. Cook them for 2 hours. Flip the ribs over and cook them for another hour.

Lay out two large double-thick sheets of heavy-duty aluminum foil. Lay a slab of ribs on each, meaty-side up. As you begin to fold the foil up around the ribs, add ¼ cup (60 ml) of the apple juice to the bottom of each package. Continue folding the foil up around the ribs, closing it into a package. Return the rib packets to the cooker for 1 hour, or until the ribs are tender when poked with a toothpick.

Remove the ribs from the foil and place them back on the grill meaty-side up. Cook them for 15 minutes more, until the ribs are firmed up. Place the ribs meaty-side down on a cutting board and use a sharp knife to cut through the slab completely at each rib. To serve, flip the ribs over, reconstructing the slabs on a platter.

Makes 4 to 6 servings

FIERY CHIPOTLE INJECTION

This one is not for the meek—chipotle is fiery and smoky and packs a big flavor punch into this injection.

⅔ cup (160 ml) chicken broth
⅓ cup (80 ml) fresh orange juice
¼ cup (80 g) honey
1 tbsp ground pure chipotle pepper
1 tsp granulated garlic
1 tsp granulated onion

In a medium bowl, combine the chicken broth, orange juice, honey, chipotle, granulated garlic, and granulated onion. With a whisk, mix everything well until blended. Cover and refrigerate the mixture for up to 1 week.

Makes about 1¼ cups (300 ml)

Chipotle Pork Roast

Not your grandma's pork roast, this is a grown-up spicy dish! Cheesy potatoes will give a nice mild contrast when served alongside.

1 boneless pork loin roast, about 3 lb (1.4 kg)
1 recipe Fiery Chipotle Injection (page 68)
Morton's Kosher Salt
Black pepper

Preheat the oven to 350°F (175°C). Lay the roast on a shallow platter and cover it loosely with plastic wrap to keep the injection from splattering.

Using a kitchen injector, inject the roast through the plastic wrap in a grid pattern at 1-in (2.5-cm) intervals and about 1 in (2.5 cm) deep, squeezing about 1 tbsp of liquid into each hole. When you have finished, flip the roast over and repeat the process until the liquid has all been used. Remove the plastic wrap. Rub the roast all over with the liquid that has accumulated on the surface. Season it with salt and pepper on all sides.

Place the roast in a shallow pan on a rack. Roast the pork for about 1 hour and 15 minutes, until the internal temperature reaches 150°F (65°C). Remove it from the oven and tent it loosely with foil. Let it rest for 10 minutes. To serve, slice the roast thinly and transfer it to a platter. Drizzle it with the pan juices, if desired.

Makes about 6 servings

BONESMOKER'S PORK INJECTION

I've been a barbecue-contest cook for over thirty years, and this is the kind of liquid that almost all the champions inject into their pork before cooking. At that level, the inside needs to be seasoned as well as the outside for a big cut of meat like this.

1 cup (240 ml) white grape juice
1 cup (240 ml) apple juice
½ cup (100 g) sugar
¼ cup (60 g) Morton's Kosher Salt
2 tbsp cider vinegar
2 tbsp Worcestershire sauce
1 tbsp granulated onion
1 tbsp granulated garlic
1 tbsp dry mustard
1 tsp cayenne

In a medium bowl, combine the grape juice, apple juice, sugar, salt, vinegar, Worcestershire, granulated onion, granulated garlic, mustard, and cayenne. With a whisk, mix everything until well blended. Cover and refrigerate the mixture for up to 1 week.

Makes about 2½ cups (600 ml)

Competition-Style Pulled Pork

This is what real barbecue is all about, and if you have never tried it, you should do so very soon. Just beware that once your friends taste this, they will want you to cook it often. This is traditionally served with fluffy white buns layered with slaw, extra sauce on the side.

> 1 whole bone-in pork butt, 7 to 8 lb (3 to 4 kg)
> 1 recipe Bonesmoker's Pork Injection (page 71)
> 1 cup (220 g) barbecue rub such as Barbecue Rub #34 (page 133)
> ¼ cup (60 ml) apple juice

A half hour before you plan to cook, trim any excess fat from the pork butt, leaving the thick fat cap intact. Lay the pork on a platter fat-side down and cover it loosely with plastic wrap to keep the injection from splattering.

Using a kitchen injector, inject the roast through the plastic wrap in a grid pattern at 1-in (2.5-cm) intervals and about 1 in (2.5 cm) deep, squeezing about 1 tbsp of liquid into each hole. When you have finished, flip the roast over and repeat the process until the liquid has all been used. Remove the plastic wrap and dry the outside of the pork with paper towels. Season it liberally on all sides with the rub, skipping the fat cap.

Prepare an outdoor grill or smoker to cook indirect at 275°F (135°C) using a combination of hickory and cherry wood for flavor. Put the butt in the cooker fat-side down and cook it for 6 to 8 hours, until it reaches an internal temperature of 160°F (73°C).

Lay out a big double-thick piece of heavy-duty aluminum foil. Put the pork butt in the middle, fat-side up. As you begin to close up the foil, pour the apple juice over the top of the butt and then seal the package, taking care not to puncture it. Return the package to the cooker for another 2 to 3 hours, until the meat reaches an internal temperature of 195°F (93°C).

Remove the package from the cooker to a baking sheet. Open the top of the foil to let the steam out and let it rest for 30 minutes. Using heavy gloves or a pair of tongs and a large fork, transfer the meat to a big pan. It will be very tender and hard to handle. Discard the juices, as they will be quite fatty. Shred the meat, discarding the fat and bones. It should just fall apart. Continue to pull the meat until it's the texture that you like. Transfer it to a platter and serve it family-style.

Makes about 12 servings

GARLICKY BUTTER INJECTION

This injection has everyone's favorite flavor combination of garlic and butter with a little herb surprise.

¾ cup (170 g) butter
6 garlic cloves, crushed
½ tsp black pepper
¼ tsp ground thyme

In a microwave-safe bowl, combine the butter, garlic, pepper, and thyme. Place it in the microwave and cook the ingredients on high for 1 minute, or until the butter has melted. Mix it well and set the butter aside to steep for 5 minutes. Return it to the microwave and cook it on high for 30 seconds more.

Strain the butter mixture through a fine sieve. Use immediately so it remains liquid and is able to flow through the injector needle.

Makes about ¾ cup (180 ml)

Garlic-Butter Chicken Breasts

These chicken breasts won't be dry and boring after they get the garlic-butter injection! They go very well with simple sides like rice pilaf and steamed broccoli.

4 boneless skinless chicken breast fillets, about 2 lb (910 g) total
1 recipe Garlicky Butter Injection (page 75)
Morton's Kosher Salt
Black pepper

Prepare an outdoor grill to cook direct over medium heat. Lay the breasts on a shallow platter and cover them loosely with plastic wrap to keep the injection from splattering.

Using a kitchen injector, inject the chicken through the plastic in a grid pattern at 1-in (2.5-cm) intervals and about ½ in (12 mm) deep, squeezing about 1 tsp of liquid into each hole. When you have finished, flip the breasts over and repeat the process until the liquid has all been used. Remove the plastic and rub the breasts all over with the liquid that has accumulated on the surface and then season them with salt and pepper on all sides.

Grill the chicken for 6 to 8 minutes, until the bottoms are golden brown. Flip the breasts over and cook them for another 6 to 8 minutes, until golden brown on the second side and the internal temperature deep inside the thickest part reaches 160°F (73°C). Transfer the chicken to a platter and tent it loosely with foil. Let it rest for 5 minutes. Serve one whole breast to each guest.

Makes 4 servings

BIG KICK INJECTION

Lots of chili powder and cayenne kick up the heat and really bring great flavor to just about anything you inject this into.

1 cup (240 ml) chicken broth
2 tbsp olive oil
Juice of ½ lemon
1 tbsp chili powder
1 tbsp granulated garlic
1 tsp cayenne
½ tsp Morton's Kosher Salt

In a small bowl, combine the chicken broth, olive oil, lemon juice, chili powder, granulated garlic, cayenne, and salt. With a whisk, mix everything until well blended. Cover and refrigerate the mixture for up to 1 week.

Makes about 1½ cups (360 ml)

Kickin' Inside-Out Chicken Wings

The big flavor kick from the inside out makes these chicken wings very special as an appetizer or main course. I serve them with the usual suspects of celery sticks and ranch or blue cheese dressing.

12 large whole fresh chicken wings, about 2½ lb (1.2 kg) total
1 recipe Big Kick Injection (page 77)
Morton's Kosher Salt

Preheat the oven to 400°F (200°C).

Using a kitchen injector, inject each wing in the drumette and center section with about 1 tbsp of the liquid. Season the wings lightly with salt. Place the wings on a rack over a baking sheet and brush them with any remaining injection liquid. If you still have any liquid left, discard it.

Cook the wings for 30 minutes. Remove the pan from the oven and flip all of the wings over. Return them to the oven for another 30 minutes, or until they have reached your desired degree of crispiness. Remove the wings from the oven and transfer them to a plate. Serve them family-style, allowing two or three wings per person.

Makes 4 to 6 servings

SWEET TEA INJECTION

In the South, everybody loves sweet tea in their glass, but it turns out to make a great injection ingredient, too.

> 2 cups (480 ml) water
> 4 black tea bags
> ⅓ cup (65 g) sugar
> Juice of 1 lemon
> 1 tbsp Morton's Kosher Salt
> ½ tsp white pepper

In a small saucepan, bring the water just to a boil. Remove it from the heat, add the tea bags, cover, and let them steep for 15 minutes. Remove the tea bags and discard them. Add the sugar, lemon juice, salt, and pepper. Mix them well and let them cool to room temperature before using. Cover and refrigerate the mixture for up to 1 week.

Makes about 2 cups (480 ml)

Sweet Tea Turkey Breast

This is a fun way to change things up. See if anyone can figure out the secret ingredient. I like to serve Southern sweet potato casserole and glazed carrots with this.

> 1 bone-in turkey breast, about 6 lb (2.5 kg)
> 1 recipe Sweet Tea Injection (page 81)
> Morton's Kosher Salt
> Black pepper

Prepare an outdoor grill to cook indirect at 325°F (165°C). Lay the turkey on a shallow platter and cover it loosely with plastic wrap to keep the injection from splattering.

Using a kitchen injector, inject the turkey through the plastic in a grid pattern at 1-in (2.5-cm) intervals and about 1 in (2.5 cm) deep, squeezing about 2 tbsp of liquid into each hole. Continue injecting it on all sides until the liquid has all been used. Remove the plastic wrap and rub the turkey all over with the liquid that has accumulated on the surface and then season it with salt and pepper on all sides. Place the turkey in a disposable or other grill-safe pan on the cooking grate.

Cover and cook the turkey for about 2 hours, until it reaches an internal temperature of 160°F (73°C) deep in the thickest part of the meat. Remove the pan from the grill and tent the turkey loosely with foil. Let it rest for 20 minutes. Slice it to serve and drizzle it with the pan juices, if desired.

Makes about 8 servings

SCOTTIE'S WHISKEY-BUTTER INJECTION

This is a bold-flavored mixture that really tastes of whiskey. If you're serving kids, you can substitute apple juice, but I think the grown-ups are going to love it as-is.

2 cups (455 g) butter
1 cup (240 ml) Tennessee whiskey
1 tbsp barbecue rub such as Barbecue Rub #34 (page 133)
1 tbsp finely ground white pepper
1 tbsp finely ground black pepper
1 tbsp Morton's Kosher Salt
1 tbsp granulated garlic
1 tbsp granulated onion
1 tbsp dry mustard
1 tsp cayenne

In a medium saucepan over medium heat, melt the butter. Add the whiskey, rub, white pepper, black pepper, salt, granulated garlic, granulated onion, mustard, and cayenne. Cook the mixture for 2 to 3 minutes, stirring often, until it's well blended. Let it cool completely before using. Cover and refrigerate the mixture for up to 1 week.

Makes about 3 cups (720 ml)

Scottie's Deep-Fried Turkey

These recipes come from my friend Scottie Johnson. Scottie won the Jack Daniel's World Barbecue Championship in 2006. Scottie and his beautiful daughters, Zoe and Lexi, run Cancer Sucks Chicago and CorlissFoundation.com in memory of their mom, who left us way too early. You'll need a turkey fryer like those at the hardware store and a lot of peanut oil. I like to serve this with dirty rice and garlic bread.

> 1 fully defrosted frozen turkey, about 15 lb (7 kg)
> 1 recipe Scottie's Whiskey-Butter Injection (page 83)
> Seasoned salt
> Peanut oil

Remove all the giblets and the neck from the turkey and tuck the wings behind the neck. Pat the turkey dry inside and out with paper towels. Lay the turkey on a shallow platter and cover it loosely with plastic wrap to keep the injection from splattering.

Using a kitchen injector, inject the turkey through the plastic deeply into the muscles at 2-in (5-cm) intervals, in a grid pattern, squeezing about 2 tbsp of the liquid into each hole. Continue until you've done all the parts of the turkey and you've used all of the liquid. Season the turkey inside and out with seasoned salt.

Prepare the turkey fryer per the manufacturer's instructions and fill with peanut oil. Be sure not to overfill the pot; you'll need to fit the turkey in there, too. Bring the oil temperature to 325°F (165°C). Gently ease the turkey into the oil. Return the temperature to 325°F (165°C) and hold it between there and 350°F (175°C) for 3 minutes per 1 lb (455 g), or until the internal temperature deep in the turkey thigh reaches 180°F (83°C).

Remove the turkey to drain over newspaper and let it rest for 20 minutes. Carve and arrange it on a platter to serve.

Makes about 12 servings

FULL-THROTTLE BEEF INJECTION

This injection is packed with beefy flavors and delivers full-throttle fired-up flavor. It's really intense and not suited for anything but beef, but you might try it as a braising liquid on pot roast day.

2 cups (480 ml) beef broth
1 tbsp soy sauce
2 tsp Louisiana hot sauce
1 tsp granulated onion
1 tsp granulated garlic
1 tsp chili powder
½ tsp white pepper

In a small saucepan over medium-high heat, bring the beef broth to a simmer. Lower the heat to maintain a medium simmer and cook it for 15 minutes, stirring occasionally. Add the soy sauce, hot sauce, granulated onion, granulated garlic, chili powder, and pepper. Return the mixture to a simmer and cook it for another 15 minutes, until it is reduced to 1 cup (240 ml). Transfer the liquid to a bowl to cool. Cover and refrigerate the mixture for up to 1 week.

Makes about 1 cup (240 ml)

Full-Throttle Tri-Tip

Half of the people in the United States love tri-tip, and the other half don't even know what it is. If you're in the slighted half, ask the butcher and maybe you'll get lucky and find one. If you like sirloin flavor, you are going to become a fan. Slice it thin and serve it on crusty bread with french fries.

> **1 whole USDA Choice beef tri-tip, about 2½ lb (1.2 kg)**
> **1 recipe Full-Throttle Beef Injection (facing page)**
> **Morton's Kosher Salt**
> **Black pepper**

Prepare an outdoor grill to cook direct over medium heat. Lay the tri-tip on a shallow platter and cover it loosely with plastic wrap to keep the injection from splattering.

Using a kitchen injector, inject the beef through the plastic in a grid pattern at 1-in (2.5-cm) intervals and about 1 in (2.5 cm) deep. Inject about ½ tsp into each hole until all of the liquid has been used. Season the tri-tip with salt and pepper and place it on the grill.

Grill the tri-tip for 8 to 10 minutes, until the beef is well browned on the bottom. Flip the tri-tip over and cook it for another 8 to 10 minutes, until the second side is well browned. Continue cooking and flipping it every 2 to 3 minutes, until the tri-tip is well browned on all sides and has reached an internal temperature of 125°F (50°C) for medium-rare. Remove the tri-tip from the grill and tent it loosely with aluminum foil. Let it rest for 10 minutes. Slice it thinly against the grain to serve.

Makes 4 servings

BIG BOLD BEEF INJECTION

This coffee-spiked injection is just right for the long-cooking cuts of beef. Brisket, short ribs, pot roast, or even a prime rib will all do very well with these flavors.

> 1½ cups (360 ml) strong beef broth
> ½ cup (120 ml) strong coffee
> 2 tbsp Worcestershire sauce
> 2 tbsp soy sauce
> 1 tsp Morton's Kosher Salt
> 1 tsp granulated garlic
> 1 tsp granulated onion
> 1 tsp finely ground black pepper

In a medium bowl, combine the beef broth, coffee, Worcestershire, soy sauce, salt, granulated garlic, granulated onion, and pepper. With a whisk, mix everything until well blended. Cover and refrigerate the mixture for up to 1 week.

Makes about 2¼ cups (540 ml)

Great-Flavor Barbecue Brisket

Injecting a brisket is kind of a new thing, but it really enhances the flavor and helps keep it from getting dry. My serving method is old school—slicing both muscles at the same time. Serve this with the traditional sides of beans, potato salad, and white bread.

> 1 whole USDA Choice brisket, 12 to 15 lb (5.4 to 6.8 kg)
> 1 recipe Big Bold Beef Injection (facing page)
> Barbecue rub such as Barbecue Rub #34 (page 133)

About an hour before you plan to cook, prepare the brisket by trimming most of the fat from the pockets on the sides. Trim any loose or hanging edges. The fat cap should remain mostly intact, but if there is an extremely thick spot, trim it to even things out. Lay the brisket fat-side down on a baking sheet and cover it loosely with plastic wrap to keep the injection from splattering. Set aside ¼ cup (60 ml) of the injection liquid to be used later.

Using a kitchen injector, inject the brisket through the plastic in a grid pattern at 1-in (2.5-cm) intervals and about 1 in (2.5 cm) deep, squeezing about 2 tbsp of liquid into each hole. Keep injecting until you've used all of the liquid. Remove the plastic wrap and dry the outside of the brisket with a paper towel. Season it liberally with the barbecue rub on all sides except the fat cap.

Prepare an outdoor smoker or grill capable of cooking slowly to cook indirect at 235°F (115°C) using oak wood for flavor. Place the brisket in the cooker fat-side down. After 6 hours, flip the brisket over and continue cooking until the internal temperature reaches 180°F (83°C) deep in the flat muscle, another 3 to 4 hours.

Lay out a double-thick piece of heavy-duty aluminum foil. Place the brisket on it, fat-side up. Bring the edges of the foil up and add the reserved ¼ cup (60 ml) injection liquid to the bottom of the package. Continue wrapping the foil up around the brisket to enclose it. Place the package back in the cooker until the internal temperature deep in the flat muscle of the brisket reaches 195°F (93°C) and a toothpick pushed into the meat slides in and out very easily. This will take about 2 hours more, but please use a thermometer to get it done just right.

Remove the package to a baking sheet and let it rest for 1 hour at room temperature. Unwrap the foil and transfer the brisket to a cutting board. Reserve any juice that has accumulated in the foil and defat it if needed. Using a long sharp knife, trim away all the fat, including the fat cap. Slice the whole brisket across the grain about ½ in (12 mm) thick. Transfer the slices to a platter and drizzle them with the reserved juice to serve.

Makes about 15 servings

BRINES

Brining is an ancient technique originally used to preserve food,

but in the modern kitchen it's most often used to flavor and add moisture to meat and seafood before cooking. The science is easily found if you're the inquisitive type, but for our purposes I'll skip it here and cut right to a simple explanation.

The meat is submerged in a salty liquid and the salt is drawn into the meat, taking with it liquid and the taste of any herbs, spices, or other flavorings that have been added. The meat will take on up to 20 percent additional liquid weight and will resist losing it during cooking. The end result is a juicy product with the added flavors deep inside. Even if you overcook the food a bit, the brine will keep it moist. This is why brining is so popular with home cooks on Thanksgiving. Nobody likes a dry turkey, and brining will help keep it moist.

There is also limited tenderizing that occurs and that's a nice bonus; but for me, brining is all about flavor and juiciness. Any salt will work for brining, but you should avoid additives like iodine. The ratio of salt to water for my brines is 8½ oz (240 g) salt for every 1 gl (3.8 L) water.

You can measure 240 g for all the common brands of salt, but each volume measure will be different. Let me say that again: The common brands are all the same by weight but not by volume. Got it? See my discussion of salt on page 14. All of my recipes in this book call for Morton's Kosher Salt. It weighs approximately 8½ oz (240 g) per 1 cup, but not all salt does, so if you are going to substitute you will have to weigh your salt. This may sound nit-picky, but it's important and necessary to brine properly. If your brine doesn't have enough salt, it won't carry the moisture and flavor into the meat no matter how long it soaks. If it's too salty, it will carry into the meat faster than my ratio and the meat will be too salty when cooked.

Over-brined meat also takes on a texture that I compare to lunchmeat, and it's not very pleasant in freshly cooked foods. This may make it sound like brining is all about the salt, and that's because it is. If you are sensitive to salt, you probably should skip brining altogether or at least limit your consumption. Most brines also contain sugar or other sweeteners in an amount about equal to the salt. This helps balance the salty flavor and adds a nice sweetness to the meat.

Most brines also contain additional flavoring ingredients, such as onion, garlic, carrots, celery, peppercorns, citrus, and almost always some herbs. To combine all these ingredients well, most brines are heated and cooked until well blended. But then they must always be chilled to a temp of 40°F (4°C) before adding them to the meat. So it's best to make your brine well ahead of the time you will need it.

A common and helpful trick is to heat half of the liquid with the salt, sugar, and flavoring ingredients and cook until they're well blended. Then combine the hot mixture with the rest of the liquid in a cold state (such as ice water). This helps to cool it down, but you'll still need to get the brine fully chilled to 40°F (4°C) before using. No exceptions. Making a brine a couple of days ahead is just fine as long as you keep it cold, but never ever re-use a brine after there has been meat soaked in it.

Brining is best used for lean cuts of meat that tend to dry out when cooking, such as chicken and turkey breasts and certain cuts of pork. It also works well for salmon and other firm cuts of fish. The simple rule of thumb is that the thicker the piece of meat, the longer it will need to brine. For pork chops, a few hours of soaking works, but a turkey needs a few days. The recipes here will guide you.

Be careful not to buy "enhanced" meats for brining. These are essentially prebrined and they will become too salty if you brine them again. Look for natural meat with no additives for best results.

This chapter begins with a basic and very simple brine recipe. After that, the more elaborate recipes will have icons next to them suggesting which foods they are best suited for, followed by a complete recipe utilizing the brine. Brining is a tool that many cooks really rely on, so give it a try to enjoy the great flavors it produces.

THE BASIC BRINE

Simple Meat Brine

This is the simplest of brines, but it works as well as the complex versions. Use this and your food will be juicy and tasty.

2 cups (480 ml) water, plus 2 cups (480 ml) ice water
¼ cup (60 g) Morton's Kosher Salt
¼ cup (50 g) sugar

In a medium saucepan over medium heat, combine 2 cups (480 ml) water, salt, and sugar. Mix them well. Bring the mixture to a simmer, stirring often. Cook it for 1 to 2 minutes, until the salt and sugar are dissolved. Add the ice water to a large bowl. Pour the hot brine over the ice water. With a large spoon, mix well until everything is blended. Refrigerate the brine for at least 2 hours, until well chilled. Use it immediately or keep it refrigerated for up to 1 week.

Makes about 1 qt (960 ml)

SWEET SWINE BRINE

This brine is sweet and savory, using granulated onion and garlic that dissolve easily and impart a great flavor deep into the meat. It's perfect for any cut of pork or chicken and it's great for salmon. If you like a little heat, just add some cayenne.

2 cups (480 ml) water, plus 2 cups (480 ml) ice water
¼ cup (60 g) Morton's Kosher Salt
¼ cup (50 g) Sugar In The Raw or other raw sugar
1 tbsp granulated onion
1 tbsp granulated garlic
1½ tsp black pepper

In a medium saucepan over medium heat, combine the 2 cups (480 ml) water, salt, raw sugar, granulated onion, granulated garlic, and pepper. Mix them well. Bring the mixture to a simmer, stirring often. Cook it for 1 to 2 minutes, until the salt and sugar are dissolved. Add the ice water to a large bowl. Pour the hot brine over the ice water. With a large spoon, mix well until everything is blended. Refrigerate the brine for at least 2 hours, until well chilled. Use it immediately or keep it refrigerated for up to 1 week.

Makes about 1 qt (960 ml)

Tasty Fried Pork Chops

Brining isn't for grilling and broiling alone. We all like our fried pork chops juicy and tasty, so brining is the perfect little trick. I always serve these with potatoes au gratin and the guests never complain.

> 4 bone-in pork chops, about ¾ in (2 cm) thick
> 1 recipe cold Sweet Swine Brine (facing page)
> ½ cup (65 g) all-purpose flour
> ½ tsp Morton's Kosher Salt
> ½ tsp black pepper
> 2 eggs
> 1 cup (115 g) dry bread crumbs
> Peanut oil

Place the chops in a large heavy-duty zip-top bag. Pour the brine over them. Seal the bag, squeezing out as much air as possible. Place the bag in a pan or bowl in case of leakage and refrigerate it for 3 to 4 hours, occasionally moving the chops around within the bag.

On a flat plate, combine the flour, salt, and pepper. In a shallow bowl, lightly beat the eggs with 1 tbsp water. Place the bread crumbs on a flat plate. Remove the chops from the brine and dry them well.

Preheat a large skillet with ¼ in (6 mm) of peanut oil. Dredge the chops one at a time in the flour, coating them well and shaking off any excess. Dip each chop in the egg mixture, coating them well and shaking off any excess. Dredge each chop in the bread crumbs, coating them well and shaking off any excess. When the oil is hot, place all the chops in the skillet. If they won't fit without crowding, just do it in two batches.

Cook them for 5 to 6 minutes, until they're deep golden brown. Flip the chops over and cook them for another 5 to 6 minutes, until they're deep golden brown on the second side and reach an internal temperature of 150°F (65°C) deep in the center of the meat. Transfer the chops to a plate lined with paper towels to drain. Let them rest for 5 minutes. Serve one chop to each diner.

Makes 4 servings

MAPLE BRINE

All brines need a sweetener to temper the salt, and maple syrup turns this one into a very special treat. Be sure to use real maple syrup. It's a little pricey, but the true maple flavor is well worth it.

2 cups (480 ml) water, plus 2 cups (480 ml) ice water
½ cup (120 ml) pure maple syrup
¼ cup (60 g) Morton's Kosher Salt
1 tbsp vanilla extract
1 tsp granulated onion
1 tsp black pepper
½ tsp cinnamon
¼ tsp ground nutmeg

In a medium saucepan over medium heat, combine the 2 cups (480 ml) water, maple syrup, salt, vanilla, granulated onion, pepper, cinnamon, and nutmeg. Mix them well. Bring the mixture to a simmer, stirring often. Cook it for 1 to 2 minutes, until the salt and syrup are dissolved. Add the ice water to a large bowl. Pour the hot brine over the ice water. With a large spoon, mix well until everything is blended. Refrigerate the brine for at least 2 hours, until well chilled. Use it immediately or keep it refrigerated for up to 1 week.

Makes about 1 qt (960 ml)

Maple-Brined Pork Chops

There is something really special about the combination of grilled pork and maple syrup, and these are a great example. I think the chops are great paired with grilled sweet corn and grilled Texas toast.

> 4 bone-in pork chops, about ¾ in (2 cm) thick
> 1 recipe cold Maple Brine (page 99)
> 2 tbsp pure maple syrup

Place the chops in a large heavy-duty zip-top bag. Pour the brine over them. Seal the bag, squeezing out as much air as possible. Place the bag in a pan or bowl in case of leakage and refrigerate it for 3 to 4 hours, occasionally moving the chops around within the bag.

Prepare an outdoor grill to cook direct over medium heat. Remove the chops from the brine and rinse them under cold water. Dry the chops well. Place them on the grill and cook them for 5 to 6 minutes, until they're golden brown. Flip them over and cook them for another 5 to 6 minutes, until they reach an internal temperature of 150°F (65°C) deep in the center. Remove them to a plate and brush each chop with the maple syrup on all sides. Serve one chop to each guest.

Makes 4 servings

CRANBERRY BRINE

This is a perfect holiday brine with distinct flavors from the fruit juices. It really delivers the cranberry flavor and is delicious with pork roasts, chops, or even a turkey breast.

2 cups (480 ml) cranberry juice

1 cup (240 ml) fresh orange juice

¼ cup (50 g) packed brown sugar

¼ cup (60 ml) molasses

¼ cup (60 g) Morton's Kosher Salt

2 garlic cloves, crushed

2 sprigs fresh thyme

1 bay leaf

1 tsp black pepper

¼ tsp cinnamon

1 cup (240 ml) ice water

In a medium saucepan over medium heat, combine the cranberry juice, orange juice, brown sugar, molasses, salt, garlic, thyme, bay leaf, pepper, and cinnamon. Mix them well. Bring the mixture to a simmer, stirring often. Cook it for 1 to 2 minutes, until the salt and sugar are dissolved. Add the ice water to a large bowl. Pour the hot brine over the ice water. With a large spoon, mix well until everything is blended. Refrigerate the brine for at least 2 hours, until well chilled. Use it immediately or keep it refrigerated for up to 1 week.

Makes about 1 qt (960 ml)

Holiday Pork Roast

A pork roast is the perfect partner for the Cranberry Brine, and your house will smell like the holidays while it cooks. I like to serve this with a long list of traditional favorites like mashed potatoes, dressing, green bean casserole, and a Jell-O salad.

> 1 boneless pork loin roast, 3 to 4 lb (1.5 to 2 kg)
> 1 recipe cold Cranberry Brine (facing page)
> 1 medium onion, quartered

Place the roast in a large heavy-duty zip-top bag. Pour the brine over the roast. Seal the bag, squeezing out as much air as possible. Place the bag in a pan in case of leakage and refrigerate it for 12 to 15 hours, occasionally moving the roast around within the bag.

Preheat the oven to 350°F (175°C). Remove the roast from the brine and rinse it under cold water. Dry the roast well. Using butcher string, tie the roast firmly in four or five evenly spaced places. Place the roast on a rack in a shallow roasting pan. Lay the onion quarters around the roast. Roast it for about 1 hour and 20 minutes, until the internal temperature reaches 150°F (65°C) deep in the center. Remove it from the oven and tent it loosely with foil. Let it rest for 10 minutes. To serve, remove the string and slice the roast thinly.

Makes 4 to 6 servings

TASTY BRINE

The great exotic flavors in this brine come from substituting soy sauce for the salt and reinforcing that with additional Asian ingredients. Add a little extra sriracha if you dare.

¾ cup (180 ml) water, plus 1 cup (240 ml) ice water
¼ cup (60 ml) soy sauce
1 tbsp Morton's Kosher Salt
2 tbsp Sugar In The Raw or other raw sugar
Juice of ½ lime
2 garlic cloves, crushed
1½ tsp sesame oil
1½ tsp sriracha sauce
1 tsp granulated onion

In a medium saucepan over medium heat, combine the ¾ cup (180 ml) water, soy sauce, salt, raw sugar, lime juice, garlic, sesame oil, sriracha, and granulated onion. Mix them well. Bring the mixture to a simmer, stirring often. Cook it for 1 to 2 minutes, until the salt and sugar are dissolved. Add the ice water to a large bowl. Pour the hot brine over the ice water. With a large spoon, mix well until everything is blended. Refrigerate the brine for at least 2 hours, until well chilled. Use it immediately or keep it refrigerated for up to 1 week.

Makes about 2¼ cups (540 ml)

Sandi's Big Salad

Sandi is the love of my life, and she makes wonderful big salads at home using whatever leftover meats I have in the refrigerator. So I figured I'd give her some chicken breasts and my Tasty Brine and have her create a recipe for me. I think she knocked it out of the park! She serves this with garlic breadsticks.

2 boneless skinless chicken breast fillets, about 1 lb (455 g) total
1 recipe cold Tasty Brine (facing page)

Salad

10 oz (280 g) mixed salad greens, such as mesclun, arugula,
   red leaf, romaine, or baby spinach
1 cup (120 g) matchstick carrots
1 cup (135 g) blue cheese crumbles
20 grape tomatoes, halved
½ cup (70 g) dried cranberries
½ cup (60 g) chopped pecans
3 scallions, white and green parts thinly sliced

Dressing

1 cup (320 g) jalapeño pepper jelly
½ cup (120 ml) fresh orange juice
¼ cup (60 ml) olive oil
2 tbsp red wine vinegar
½ tsp Morton's Kosher Salt

8 slices bacon, cooked crisp and crumbled

With a meat mallet, pound the breast fillets until they are evenly about ¾ in (2 cm) thick. Place the fillets in a large heavy-duty zip-top bag. Pour the brine over them. Seal the bag, squeezing out as much air as possible. Place the bag in a pan or bowl in case of leakage and refrigerate it for 2 to 3 hours, occasionally moving the chicken around within the bag.

Preheat the broiler to cook on high. Remove the chicken from the brine and rinse it under cold water. Dry the chicken thoroughly. Place it on a baking sheet or broiler pan under the broiler. Cook it for 6 to 8 minutes, until the tops are golden brown. Flip the chicken over and cook it for another 6 to 8 minutes, until the internal temperature deep in the center of the meat reaches 160°F (73°C). Remove the chicken to a cutting board to rest.

To make the salad: In a large bowl, combine the greens, carrots, blue cheese, tomatoes, cranberries, pecans, and scallions. Toss to mix them well.

To make the dressing: In the pitcher of a blender, combine the pepper jelly, orange juice, olive oil, vinegar, and salt. Blend them on high speed for about 1 minute until combined.

Cut the chicken into pieces about ¾ in (2 cm) square. Add them to the salad bowl and toss to mix. Pour about three-quarters of the dressing over the salad and toss well. Taste and add the remaining salad dressing if desired. Toss it well and serve it with the bacon scattered over the top.

Makes 4 servings

LEMON-PEPPER QUICKY BRINE

Lemon-pepper is a great flavor added to a brine, bringing a little spicy citrus kick to whatever you soak in it. Chicken breast is the perfect match, but a slab of salmon would go pretty well, too.

2 cups (480 ml) water, plus 2 cups (480 ml) ice water
¼ cup (60 g) Morton's Kosher Salt
¼ cup (50 g) Sugar In The Raw or other raw sugar
Zest and juice of 2 lemons
1 tbsp black pepper
1 tbsp granulated garlic
1 tsp granulated onion

In a medium saucepan over medium heat, combine the 2 cups (480 ml) water, salt, raw sugar, lemon zest, lemon juice, pepper, granulated garlic, and granulated onion. Mix them well. Bring the mixture to a simmer, stirring often. Cook it for 1 to 2 minutes, until the salt and sugar are dissolved. Add the ice water to a large bowl. Pour the hot brine over the ice water. With a large spoon, mix well until everything is blended. Refrigerate the brine for at least 2 hours, until well chilled. Use it immediately or keep it refrigerated for up to 1 week.

Makes about 1 qt (960 ml)

Broiled Lemon-Pepper Chicken Breast

Boneless skinless chicken breasts can be dry, but they get great help from brining. The lemon-pepper flavor makes these very special and versatile. I serve these with a rice pilaf, on a sandwich, or sliced on top of a Caesar salad.

4 boneless skinless chicken breast fillets, about 2 lb (910 g) total
1 recipe cold Lemon-Pepper Quicky Brine (facing page)
Black pepper
1 lemon, cut into wedges

With a meat mallet, pound the breast fillets until they are evenly about ¾ in (2 cm) thick. Place the fillets in a large heavy-duty zip-top bag. Pour the brine over them. Seal the bag, squeezing out as much air as possible. Place the bag in a pan or bowl in case of leakage and refrigerate it for 2 to 3 hours, occasionally moving the chicken around within the bag.

Preheat the broiler to cook on high. Remove the chicken from the brine and rinse it under cold water. Dry the chicken thoroughly. Season it lightly on all sides with pepper. Place the chicken on a baking sheet or broiler pan under the broiler. Cook it for 6 to 8 minutes, until the tops are golden brown. Flip the chicken over and cook it for another 6 to 8 minutes, until the internal temperature deep in the center of the meat reaches 160°F (73°C). Remove the chicken to a plate and let rest for 5 minutes. Serve one fillet per person, with the lemon wedges.

Makes 4 servings

THREE-DAY TURKEY BRINE

If the turkey at your house is dry and you haven't discovered brining, this would be a great way for you to get started. It will change your family's attitude toward the big bird forever.

> 2 qt (2 L) apple juice
> 2 qt (2 L) orange juice
> 2 cups (480 g) Morton's Kosher Salt
> 1 cup (320 g) honey
> 1 cup (200 g) Sugar In The Raw or other raw sugar
> 8 sprigs fresh thyme
> ¼ cup (10 g) peppercorns
> 1 gl (3.8 L) ice water

In a large pot over medium-high heat, combine the apple juice, orange juice, salt, honey, raw sugar, thyme, and peppercorns. Mix them well and cook, stirring often, until the mixture reaches a boil. Lower the heat and simmer for about 5 minutes, stirring often, until the sugar and salt are dissolved. Add the ice water to a large container. Pour the hot brine over the ice water. With a large spoon, mix well until everything is blended. Refrigerate the brine for at least 4 hours, and preferably overnight, until well chilled. Use it immediately or keep it refrigerated for up to 1 week.

Makes about 2 gl (7.5 L)

A Very Juicy Thanksgiving Turkey

The brine process that most home cooks are familiar with is this ritualistic three-day brine of the turkey leading up to Thanksgiving. It's saved a lot of birds from being dry and tasteless and made a lot of happy Thanksgivings.

    1 fully defrosted frozen turkey, 12 to 15 lb (5.4 to 6.8 kg)
    1 recipe cold Three-Day Turkey Brine (facing page)
    1 lemon, halved
    1 small onion, quartered
    6 sprigs fresh thyme
    Vegetable oil

Three days before you plan to cook, place the turkey in a large oven-cooking bag. Pour the brine into the bag with the turkey. Tie it at the top, squeezing out as much air as possible. Put it in a new plastic 5-gl (18.8-L) bucket in case of leakage and refrigerate it for 3 days, occasionally moving the turkey around inside the bag.

Ninety minutes before you plan to cook, remove the turkey from the bag and rinse it well inside and out under cold running water. Dry the turkey well, inside and out, and place it on a large platter. Fill a large heavy-duty zip-top bag with ice cubes. Place the ice pack directly on the breast of the turkey, covering as much meat as possible. Let it rest for 1 hour at room temperature.

Preheat the oven to 325°F (165°C) or prepare an outdoor grill to cook indirect over medium-low heat. Remove the ice pack and dry the turkey well. Place the lemon, onion, and thyme in the cavity of the turkey. Tuck the wing tips back behind its neck. Rub the turkey all over with a light coat of vegetable oil. For cooking on the grill, place the turkey directly on the cooking grate, breast-side up. For cooking in the oven, place the turkey on a rack in a low-sided roasting pan in the oven.

Cook the turkey for 3 to 3½ hours, until it is golden brown and has reached an internal temperature of 160°F (73°C) deep in the breast meat and 180°F (83°C) deep in the thigh meat. Remove it to a large platter and tent it loosely with foil. Let it rest for 20 minutes. Carve the turkey and transfer it to a platter to serve.

Makes about 12 servings

DR. BBQ'S CORNED BEEF BRINE

Corned beef is really just brined beef with a bit of curing salt added to preserve it and give it that iconic red color. That great corned beef flavor comes from pickling spice, which is a blend of ingredients commonly used in pickling, such as whole mustard seeds, coriander seeds, allspice, peppercorns, celery seeds, crumbled bay leaves, ginger, mace, cloves, and cinnamon.

2 qt (2 L) water, plus 2 qt (2 L) ice water
2 cups (400 g) Morton's Tender Quick
½ cup (100 g) Sugar In The Raw or other raw sugar
⅓ cup (10 g) pickling spice
10 garlic cloves, coarsely chopped
2 tbsp whole peppercorns

In a large pot over medium-high heat, combine the 2 qt (2 L) water, Tender Quick, raw sugar, pickling spice, garlic, and peppercorns. Mix them well. Bring the mixture to a simmer, stirring often, for 3 to 4 minutes, until the Tender Quick and sugar are dissolved. Add the ice water to a large pot. Pour the hot brine over the ice water. With a large spoon, mix well until everything is blended. Refrigerate the brine for at least 4 hours, until well chilled. Use it immediately or keep it refrigerated for up to 1 week.

Makes about 1 gl (3.8 L)

Housemade Corned Beef

Making corned beef at home is really pretty simple, and it's much better than the store-bought stuff. You just need to start a week before you want to eat it. I like to do it around St. Patrick's Day so my corned beef is the envy of the neighborhood.

1 USDA Choice beef brisket flat, about 8 lb (3.6 kg), with a thin layer of fat on top

1 recipe cold Dr. BBQ's Corned Beef Brine (page 113)

1 large onion, quartered

4 garlic cloves

1 tbsp pickling spice

6 large carrots, peeled and cut into 2-in (5-cm) pieces

3 large russet potatoes, peeled and quartered

Seven days before you plan to cook, place the brisket in a large oven-cooking bag, then in a pan large enough to hold it all in case of leakage. Pour the brine into the bag. Tie it at the top, squeezing out as much air as possible. Refrigerate it for 7 days, flipping the whole package over every day and massaging the brisket for a few seconds to help the penetration of the brine.

After 7 days, remove the brisket from the brine and rinse it well under cold water. Add it to a large pot and cover it with cold water by 2 in (5 cm). Add the onion, garlic, and pickling spice. Stir the pot.

Over medium-high heat, bring the water to a low boil. Cover and cook the brisket for 1½ hours. Add the carrots and potatoes. Cover and cook the brisket for another hour, and then check the beef for doneness by poking it with a large fork. When done properly, the tines of the fork should slide in and out of the meat very easily. If it's not done, just cook it for another 30 minutes and check again. Repeat until the corned beef reaches your desired degree of tenderness.

Remove the corned beef to a cutting board and tent it loosely with foil. Let it rest for 5 minutes. With a slotted spoon, remove the potatoes and carrots to a bowl. Slice the corned beef thinly against the grain. Transfer it to a platter and serve it with the carrots and potatoes.

Makes about 10 servings

SHORT SHRIMP BRINE

This simple brine is perfect for short-term brining of small pieces and it goes very well with mild flavors like shrimp, salmon, or chicken breast.

> 1 cup (240 ml) water, plus 1 cup (240 ml) ice water
> 2 tbsp Morton's Kosher Salt
> 2 tbsp Sugar In The Raw or other raw sugar
> 1 tsp white pepper
> 1 tsp granulated garlic
> 1 tsp granulated onion

In a medium saucepan over medium heat, combine the 1 cup (240 ml) water, salt, raw sugar, pepper, granulated garlic, and granulated onion. Mix them well. Bring the mixture to a simmer, stirring often. Cook it for 1 to 2 minutes, until the salt and sugar are dissolved. Add the ice water to a medium bowl. Pour the hot brine over the ice water. With a large spoon, mix well until everything is blended. Refrigerate the brine for at least 2 hours, until well chilled. Use it immediately or keep it refrigerated for up to 1 week.

Makes about 2 cups (480 ml)

Tasty Grilled Shrimp Cocktail

Brining shrimp before grilling gives them great flavor. I serve my shrimp in martini glasses with the homemade cocktail sauce on top and a lemon slice on the rim.

> 1 lb (455 g) jumbo shrimp, peeled and deveined
> 1 recipe cold Short Shrimp Brine (facing page)
> 1 tsp paprika

Soak bamboo skewers in water for 1 hour. Meanwhile, place the shrimp in a heavy-duty zip-top bag. Pour the brine over them. Seal the bag, squeezing out as much air as possible. Place the bag in a pan or bowl in case of leakage and refrigerate it for 20 minutes, occasionally moving the shrimp around within the bag. Do not brine the shrimp for longer than 20 minutes.

Prepare an outdoor grill to cook direct over medium-high heat. Remove the shrimp from the brine and rinse them thoroughly under cold water. Thread the shrimp five or six to a skewer. Insert a second skewer parallel to the original to keep the shrimp from spinning as you flip them. Dry the shrimp well and then sprinkle them lightly with the paprika on both sides to encourage browning.

Place the shrimp skewers on the grill. Cook them for 3 to 4 minutes, until they are golden brown on the bottom. Flip the skewers over and cook them for another 3 to 4 minutes, until the shrimp are golden brown on the second side and opaque throughout. Remove them to a platter. Let them cool for 5 minutes. Remove the shrimp from the skewers and serve four or five to each guest.

Makes 4 servings

HOT-SMOKED SALMON BRINE

The trick to cooking great smoked salmon is brining. This recipe imparts rich flavor and gives any type of salmon that firm texture that we all love.

> 1 cup (240 ml) water, plus 1 cup (240 ml) ice water
> 1½ tbsp Morton's Kosher Salt
> 1 tbsp soy sauce
> 1 tbsp honey
> 1 tbsp sriracha sauce
> ½ tsp lemon pepper
> ½ tsp granulated garlic
> ½ tsp granulated onion

In a medium saucepan over medium heat, combine the 1 cup (240 ml) water, salt, soy sauce, honey, sriracha, lemon pepper, granulated garlic, and granulated onion. Mix them well. Bring the mixture to a simmer, stirring often. Cook it for 1 to 2 minutes, until the salt and honey are dissolved. Add the ice water to a medium bowl. Pour the hot brine over the ice water. With a large spoon, mix well until everything is blended. Refrigerate the brine for at least 2 hours, until well chilled. Use it immediately or keep it refrigerated for up to 1 week.

Makes about 2 cups (480 ml)

Cedar-Planked Hot-Smoked Salmon

Cold smoking is done at temps below 90°F (32°C) and that's almost impossible to do at home, so I leave that to the professionals. With a cooking plank, hot smoking is something anybody with a grill or smoker can do and the results are fabulous. This is great served warm with buttered noodles and grilled asparagus.

4 skin-on salmon fillets, about 6 oz (170 g) each
1 recipe cold Hot-Smoked Salmon Brine (page 118)

Place the fillets in a large heavy-duty zip-top bag. Pour the brine over them. Seal the bag, squeezing out as much air as possible. Place the bag in a pan or bowl in case of leakage and refrigerate it for 1 to 2 hours, occasionally moving the salmon around within the bag. Meanwhile, soak a cedar plank in water for 1 hour.

Prepare an outdoor grill to cook direct over medium heat with light alder wood for flavor. Remove the cedar plank from the water. Remove the salmon from the brine and rinse it under cold water. Dry the salmon thoroughly.

Place the salmon on the plank, spacing the fillets evenly. Place the plank directly on the grill and cook it for about 30 minutes, until it reaches an internal temperature of 135°F (60°C) and the white fat just begins to appear on the surface. Remove the plank to a baking sheet and let it rest for 5 minutes. Serve the salmon directly from the plank using a small spatula.

Makes 4 servings

RUBS

I must confess right up front that out of all the paths to great flavors that I've explored in this book, the rubs are my personal favorite. It's probably because my roots are dug deeply in the world of barbecue, where rubs are a critical component and where the term "dry rub" has its origin.

When I began my barbecue journey in the 1980s, "dry rub" was insider lingo for the blend of spices that we used to season the meat before cooking. You applied it to the meat and rubbed it in before heading to the smoker. But that exclusivity is long gone, and the term has been shortened to "rub" and is a mainstream cooking term.

Rubs are now used for seasoning everything from seafood to dessert. I'm a fan of simplicity in my cooking, so simply seasoning the meat before cooking appeals to me rather than the more involved processes of brining, injecting, or marinating. Glazes, the subject of another chapter in this book, are often used in the finishing process for dry-rubbed foods, so don't be afraid to mix a couple of my recipes together.

The key to combining those and the key to a good dry rub is balance. That's no surprise, though, because all great recipes are the result of perfectly balancing the ingredients. High-quality ingredients are also very important in achieving great flavors, so rub ingredients are no exception. Salt is pretty simple. Avoid iodized salt and you'll be on the right track. Just remember that salt crystals can vary widely in size and that can alter your measurements. For this book, I use only Morton's Kosher Salt in all of the recipes and I recommend that you do, too. If you want to experiment and learn about exotic salts, I'd recommend reading Mark Bitterman's book *Salted: A Manifesto on the World's Most Essential Mineral, with Recipes.*

After salt, the other ingredients get to be very wide-ranging and very interesting. There are many kinds of black pepper from different regions of the world, with subtle flavor differences. Ground chiles and seeds are much more diverse than can be addressed here or even in a section of shelving at the supermarket. The same is true with dried herbs and just about any other dry ingredients you'd use in a rub.

Rule number-one is to buy your ingredients as fresh as possible. This probably means not buying them at the supermarket. There are literally hundreds of great purveyors of fresh and quality spices around, so seek one out and you'll find that the difference in your food is well worth the effort. You'll also save money by buying direct, and find every item on your list with no improvising necessary. My personal favorite spice supplier is online at Penderys.com.

Rubs are the most common way of seasoning meat and can be as simple as salt and pepper or as elaborate as the number of ingredients in the cabinet. Most of my rubs keep it simple, but you should feel free to add as many of your favorite ingredients as you like. I also don't use blends or small niche ingredients in my recipes, but if you have a favorite seasoning salt or a local spice blend, just add it to the mix. You should always make the dish your own no matter what you are cooking or where you got the recipe. If you like it hot, go for it; if you like garlic, add a little more. If a little less salt is your thing, you should just omit some of it. Enjoy the recipes, but don't feel bound by them.

As with any cooking, you'll need to taste as you go when making a rub. This is a seasoning blend and it will be a bit overpowering when sampled by itself. It will also taste different when raw than it will when it's been cooked on some food. A good practice to use when blending rubs is to make a small batch and have a few small burger patties or thin-cut pork chops ready to go. When you think you have the rub tasting like you want, sprinkle a little on a burger or chop and sauté it up or give it a quick grilling to get an idea of how the rub will taste when cooked. When you've got it right, make a big batch.

The rub recipes here are stand alone. Each is followed by a recipe using the rub, but it may only use part of the batch. The rest can be saved for a month or two in a sealed container stored in a cool dry place.

This chapter begins with a basic and very simple rub recipe. After that, the more elaborate rub recipes will have icons next to them suggesting which foods they are best suited for, followed by a complete recipe utilizing the rub. Enjoy the process and the accomplishment of making your own rub with fresh ingredients. And then enjoy watching your friends and family when they taste the great flavors you've created.

THE BASIC DRY RUB

All-Purpose Kitchen Rub

This is a simple seasoning salt that works well on anything. You will use it often.

> ½ cup (120 g) Morton's Kosher Salt
> 2 tbsp granulated garlic
> 2 tbsp granulated onion
> 2 tbsp paprika
> 1 tbsp black pepper

In a small bowl, combine the salt, granulated garlic, granulated onion, paprika, and pepper. Mix them well until fully blended. Store in an airtight container in a cool dry place for up to 2 months.

Makes about ¾ cup (190 g)

PORCINE-PLEASING RUB

This is a tasty rub that's unique because of the cinnamon and coriander. I like to grind it in a food processor to make it a little finer, but it's really not necessary. It'll taste good either way.

2 tbsp Morton's Kosher Salt
2 tbsp Sugar In The raw or other raw sugar
1 tbsp paprika
1 tsp black pepper
1 tsp granulated onion
1 tsp granulated garlic
¼ tsp ground coriander
¼ tsp cinnamon
¼ tsp dried marjoram leaves
¼ tsp dried thyme leaves

In the bowl of a food processor, combine the salt, raw sugar, paprika, pepper, granulated onion, granulated garlic, coriander, cinnamon, marjoram, and thyme. Process the rub on high speed for 10 seconds, until all the ingredients are well combined. Store in an airtight container in a cool dry place for up to 2 months.

Makes about ⅓ cup (80 g)

Tasty Grilled Pork Chops

Grilled pork chops are a simple but delicious entrée that is a favorite at my house. Au gratin potatoes would be a perfect side to serve with these.

4 bone-in pork chops, about ¾ in (2 cm) thick
Olive oil
Porcine-Pleasing Rub (page 125), as needed

Prepare an outdoor grill to cook direct over medium-high heat. Brush the chops lightly all over with olive oil. Season both sides liberally with the rub. Let them rest at room temperature for 5 minutes so the seasoning can adhere to the meat.

Place the chops directly on the cooking grate. Cook them for 3 to 4 minutes, until the bottoms are golden brown. Flip the chops over and cook them for 3 to 4 minutes more, until the second sides are golden brown and the chops have reached an internal temperature of 150°F (65°C) for medium. Transfer them to a plate and tent them loosely with foil. Let them rest for 3 minutes. Serve one chop to each guest.

Makes 4 servings

COCOA GRILL RUB

I'm always on the lookout for new flavor combinations, and unsweetened cocoa really adds a new twist to a savory rub. You won't think chocolate but you will think tasty, in a *mole* kind of way.

¼ cup (25 g) unsweetened cocoa powder
1 tbsp Morton's Kosher Salt
1 tbsp Sugar In The Raw or other raw sugar
1 tsp chili powder
1 tsp black pepper
½ tsp dried orange peel
½ tsp cinnamon
Pinch of nutmeg

In the bowl of a food processor, combine the cocoa powder, salt, raw sugar, chili powder, pepper, orange peel, cinnamon, and nutmeg. Pulse them four or five times quickly, until they're well blended. Store in an airtight container in a cool dry place for up to 2 months.

Makes about ½ cup (65 g)

Cocoa-Grilled Pork Tenderloin

Pork tenderloin is a culinary blank canvas and it pairs well with just about any dry rub, including this fun one. This is wonderful served with a scoop of sweet potato puree.

2 pork tenderloins, trimmed, about 1 lb (455 g) each
Cocoa Grill Rub (page 127), as needed

Prepare an outdoor grill to cook direct over medium heat. Season the tenderloins liberally with the rub. Let them rest for 5 minutes so the rub will stick to the pork.

Place the pork on the grill and cook it for 5 to 6 minutes, until the tenderloins are golden brown on the bottom. Flip them one-third of the way over and cook them for another 5 to 6 minutes, until that side is golden brown. Flip the tenderloins to the third side and cook them for another 5 to 6 minutes, until the pork reaches an internal temperature of 150°F (65°C). Transfer the pork to a plate and tent it loosely with foil. Let the tenderloins rest for 5 minutes. Slice them thickly to serve.

Makes about 6 servings

PYRAMID BARBECUE RUB

There is a pyramid landmark in Memphis, and it's close to some of the famous barbecue joints, so I'm naming this rub after it. This is a bold rub with a lot of great flavor and color.

- **½ cup (55 g) paprika**
- **¼ cup (60 g) Morton's Kosher Salt**
- **2 tbsp chili powder**
- **2 tsp black pepper**
- **2 tsp dried oregano leaves**
- **2 tsp dried thyme leaves**
- **1 tsp ground allspice**
- **1 tsp ground coriander**

In a small bowl, combine the paprika, salt, chili powder, pepper, oregano, thyme, allspice, and coriander. Mix them well until fully blended. Store in an airtight container in a cool dry place for up to 2 months.

Makes about 1 cup (180 g)

Memphis-Style Dry-Rubbed Spareribs

Dry-rubbed barbecued ribs are a big deal in Memphis and a personal favorite of mine. Add sauce if you must, but please try them before you do and you may become a convert. These are best served with the traditional Memphis sides of beans and slaw.

> 2 slabs whole spareribs, about 4 lb (1.8 kg) each
> 1 recipe Pyramid Barbecue Rub (page 129)
> ½ cup (120 ml) cider vinegar
> ½ cup (120 ml) apple juice

At least ½ hour, and up to 4 hours, before you plan to cook, peel the membrane off the back of the ribs and cut the flap off. Trim any excess fat. Season the ribs on both sides with some of the rub. Refrigerate them until needed.

Prepare a smoker or grill to cook indirectly at 275°F (135°C) using a small amount of hickory wood for flavor. In a small bowl, combine the vinegar and apple juice. Mix them well and set aside.

Place the ribs meaty-side up on the cooking grate and close the lid. Cook them for 2 hours. Flip the ribs over and cook them for another hour. Lay out two large double-thick sheets of heavy-duty aluminum foil. Lay a slab of ribs on each, meaty-side up. As you begin to fold the foil up around the ribs, add ⅓ cup (80 ml) of the vinegar mixture to the bottom of each package. Continue folding the foil up around the ribs, closing them into a package. Return the packages to the cooker for 1 hour more, or until the ribs are tender when poked with a toothpick. Remove the ribs from the foil and place them back on the cooking grate meaty-side up. Cook them for 15 minutes, until the ribs are firmed up.

Place the ribs meaty-side down on a cutting board and use a sharp knife to cut through the slab completely at each rib. Flip the ribs back over, reconstructing the slabs on a platter. To serve, brush each slab with half of the remaining vinegar mixture and season with a liberal coating of the rub.

Makes 4 to 6 servings

BARBECUE RUB #34

If you've been following along, you know that I name some of my recipes after sports heroes. As a lifelong Chicago Bears fan, it was only a matter of time before I got around to number 34. Walter Payton was a good one, and so is this simple barbecue rub.

¼ cup (60 g) Morton's Kosher Salt
¼ cup (50 g) packed brown sugar
2 tbsp paprika
1 tbsp chili powder
1 tbsp granulated onion
1 tsp granulated garlic
2 tsp black pepper

In a small bowl, combine the salt, brown sugar, paprika, chili powder, granulated onion, granulated garlic, and pepper. Mix them well until fully blended. Store in an airtight container in a cool dry place for up to 2 months.

Makes about ¾ cup (165 g)

Slow-Smoked Pork Picnic

The pork picnic is a great cut for slow-smoked meat, with a lot of fat to render and a lot of flavor. When this is ready, I like to pull the meat from the bone and serve it with hot sauce, slow-cooked white beans, and cornbread.

> 1 whole pork picnic, about 8 lb (3.6 kg) with the skin removed
> 1 recipe Barbecue Rub #34 (page 133)
> ⅓ cup (80 ml) apple juice

Prepare a smoker or outdoor grill to cook indirect at 250°F (120°C). Season the pork liberally with the rub. Place it directly on the cooking grate and cook it for about 7 hours, until it's golden brown and reaches an internal temperature of 165°F (75°C).

Lay out a large double-thick sheet of heavy-duty aluminum foil. Place the pork on the foil and wrap it up, pouring the apple juice in before it's sealed. Return the package to the cooker for about 2 hours more, until the pork is very tender and reaches an internal temperature of 195°F (93°C).

Remove it from the cooker. Let it rest in the foil for 30 minutes. Remove the pork from the foil and transfer it to a cutting board. Pull the pork from the bone in chunks and transfer to a platter to serve.

Makes about 10 servings

SPICY BLACKENING RUB

This is a fired-up rub, but you can lighten up on the cayenne if you want to tone it down some. I prefer to use it as-is to spice up meat and serve it with some mellowing additions like cream sauce, pasta, veggies, and bread.

2 tbsp paprika
2 tbsp Morton's Kosher Salt
2 tsp granulated garlic
2 tsp granulated onion
1 tsp cayenne
1 tsp white pepper
¼ tsp ground thyme
½ tsp ground mustard

In a small bowl, combine the paprika, salt, granulated garlic, granulated onion, cayenne, pepper, thyme, and mustard. Mix them well until fully blended. Store in an airtight container in a cool dry place for up to 2 months.

Makes about ½ cup (80 g)

Blackened Chicken Po-Boy

The po-boy is the hoagie, grinder, or sub sandwich of New Orleans. In typical New Orleans fashion, their version is usually spicy and larger than life, so mine is too.

 1 recipe Spicy Blackening Rub (page 135)
 6 large boneless skinless chicken thighs, about 2 lb (910 g) total
 2 tbsp butter
 2 tbsp vegetable oil
 ½ cup (120 ml) mayonnaise
 2 large hoagie rolls
 2 cups (140 g) shredded iceberg lettuce
 2 medium tomatoes, thinly sliced

Reserve 1 tbsp of the rub and use the rest to season the chicken thighs liberally on both sides.

In a large heavy skillet over medium-high heat, melt the butter. Add the vegetable oil and mix them together. Add the thighs and cook them for 3 to 4 minutes, until they're well browned. Flip them over and cook them for another 3 to 4 minutes, until they're well browned on the second side. Flip them again, cover the pan, and cook until the thighs reach an internal temperature of 180°F (83°C). Remove them to a paper towel–lined plate.

In a small bowl, combine the mayonnaise with the reserved 1 tbsp rub. Spread the mayonnaise on both rolls. Place a handful of the lettuce on each roll. Top the lettuce with four slices of tomato. Layer three thighs on each roll. To serve, cut each sandwich in half.

Makes 4 servings

CHILI RUB

Be sure to use good-quality chili powder for this one or it will be bitter. That pretty red stuff can be used in large quantity with great results.

¼ cup (60 g) Morton's Kosher Salt
¼ cup (25 g) chili powder
2 tbsp Sugar In The Raw or other raw sugar
1 tbsp ground cumin
1 tbsp granulated garlic
1 tbsp granulated onion
1 tsp ground mustard
½ tsp cayenne (optional)

In a small bowl, combine the salt, chili powder, raw sugar, cumin, granulated garlic, granulated onion, mustard, and cayenne (if using). Mix them well until fully blended. Store in an airtight container in a cool dry place for up to 2 months.

Makes about 1 cup (125 g)

Chili-Rubbed Chicken Wings

These dry-rubbed spicy wings are a nice change from the sauced-up messy version, and they're packed with plenty of kick. Serve these with the traditional wing sides of ranch dressing and celery sticks, and add a few wedges of lime.

10 large whole fresh chicken wings, about 2 lb (910 g) total
1 recipe Chili Rub (facing page)
¼ cup (7 g) chopped fresh cilantro

Preheat the oven to 375°F (190°C). With a sharp knife, cut the tips off the chicken wings and save the tips for stock. Slash the inside of the wing joints to help them cook more evenly, but don't cut them all the way through. Season the wings liberally on all sides with the rub. Lay the wings on a baking sheet that has been coated with nonstick spray.

Bake the wings for 30 minutes. Flip the wings over and cook them for another 20 to 30 minutes, until they are golden brown and reach an internal temperature of at least 180°F (83°C). Transfer the wings to a platter and sprinkle them with the cilantro to serve.

Makes about 4 servings

ST. PETE STEAK RUB

St. Petersburg, Florida, is home for me and that's where I eat most of my steaks. Once you master the seasoning and cooking of a great steak, you'll be eating your best steaks at home, too.

¼ cup (60 g) Morton's Kosher Salt
2 tbsp Sugar In The Raw or other raw sugar
2 tbsp chili powder
1½ tbsp black pepper
1½ tbsp granulated garlic
1 tbsp granulated onion
1 tbsp ground coriander

In a small bowl, combine the salt, raw sugar, chili powder, pepper, granulated garlic, granulated onion, and coriander. Mix them well until fully blended. Store in an airtight container in a cool dry place for up to 2 months.

Makes about ¾ cup (90 g)

Perfect Porterhouse for Two

The great steakhouses all serve a porterhouse for two. It's a great way to share a romantic dinner with your honey and try both a little filet and a little strip steak. A great bottle of red wine, a couple of twice-baked potatoes, and some grilled asparagus will complete the meal beautifully.

> 1 large USDA Choice porterhouse steak, about 2 lb (910 g)
> Olive oil
> St. Pete Steak Rub (page 140), as needed
> 2 tbsp butter, at room temperature

Prepare an outdoor grill to cook direct over medium heat. Brush the steak lightly with olive oil and then season it liberally with the rub.

Place the steak directly on the cooking grate and cook it for 4 to 5 minutes, until it's well browned. Flip the steak over and cook it for another 4 to 5 minutes, until the steak is well browned on the second side. It should reach an internal temperature of 120°F (48°C) deep in the thick part of the meat near the bone for medium-rare. If necessary, move the steak to a cooler part of the grill to get it up to temperature.

Remove the steak to a platter and tent it loosely with foil. Let it rest for 5 minutes. Top it with the butter and carve it tableside to serve.

Makes 2 servings

NOTE: *The 120°F (48°C) temperature for this steak may seem a little low for medium-rare, but a big steak like this will need to rest and, while it does, the temp will rise.*

LEGEND RUB

A rub doesn't have to be complicated or use odd ingredients to be good. The right combination of the usual ingredient suspects might just make you a backyard legend.

1 tbsp Morton's Kosher Salt
1 tbsp granulated garlic
1 tbsp granulated onion
1 tbsp chili powder
1 tsp Sugar In The Raw or other raw sugar
1 tsp black pepper
¼ tsp cayenne (optional)

In a small bowl, combine the salt, granulated garlic, granulated onion, chili powder, raw sugar, pepper, and cayenne (if using). Mix them well until fully blended. Store in an airtight container in a cool dry place for up to 2 months.

Makes about ⅓ cup (70 g)

Great-Flavor Burgers

I like to make big burgers, so mine are ⅓ lb (150 g) each.

2 lb (910 g) ground chuck
Legend Rub (page 143), as needed
6 thick slices Swiss cheese
6 hard rolls, split
6 pieces romaine lettuce, about the size of the buns
6 tomato slices

Prepare an outdoor grill to cook direct over medium-high heat. Form the beef into six equal-size balls, and then form each ball into a patty, trying not to pack the meat too firmly. As you finish the patty, push your fingers into the center so it's a little thinner there. Season the burgers liberally with the rub.

Place the burgers directly on the cooking grate and cook them for 3 to 4 minutes, until golden brown on the bottom. Flip and cook them for another 3 to 4 minutes, until golden brown on the second side. Flip the burgers over again and top with the cheese. Cook them for another 1 to 2 minutes, until the burgers reach an internal temperature of 155°F (70°C) and the cheese is melted. Remove them to a platter.

Place the rolls cut-side down directly on the cooking grate and toast them for a few seconds, just until they're golden brown. Remove them to a platter. Top each roll bottom with a leaf of romaine, then add a burger. Top the burger with a slice of tomato and a roll top. Serve one burger to each person.

Makes 6 servings

BLAZING BEEF RUB

This rub is hot and spicy and not just for beef. You shouldn't mess with it unless you want your food to have a kick! It's perfect for tacos and fajitas and should be used on those days when you are just feeling a little *caliente*.

> ¼ cup (60 g) Morton's Kosher Salt
> 2 tbsp chili powder
> 2 tbsp granulated garlic
> 2 tbsp granulated onion
> 1 tsp dry mustard
> 2 tsp cayenne

In a small bowl, combine the salt, chili powder, granulated garlic, granulated onion, mustard, and cayenne. Mix them well until fully blended. Store in an airtight container in a cool dry place for up to 2 months.

Makes about ⅔ cup (130 g)

Smokin' Dry-Rubbed Steak Tacos

These are fun and fiery little soft tacos with simple toppings. Feel free to use flour tortillas if you like them better, or make a salsa instead of the tomato and scallion topping.

2 USDA Choice New York strip steaks, about ¾ in (2 cm) thick
Olive oil
Blazing Beef Rub (facing page), as needed
8 small corn tortillas
½ cup (120 ml) sour cream
2 tbsp chopped fresh cilantro
Juice of ½ lime, plus lime wedges, for serving
1 cup (115 g) finely grated Cheddar cheese
3 medium Roma tomatoes, seeded and cut into small dice
8 scallions, white and green parts thinly sliced on the bias
Hot sauce for serving

Prepare an outdoor grill to cook direct over medium-high heat. Preheat the oven to 250°F (120°C). Brush the steaks with a light coat of olive oil and season them liberally with the rub.

Wrap the tortillas in foil and place them in the oven.

Place the steaks directly on the cooking grate and cook them for 3 to 4 minutes, until they're well browned. Flip the steaks over and cook them for another 3 to 4 minutes, until they're well browned and reach an internal temperature of 125°F (50°C) for medium-rare. Transfer the steaks to a cutting board. Let them rest for 3 minutes.

Meanwhile, in a small bowl, stir together the sour cream, cilantro, and lime juice.

Slice the steaks thinly on the bias. Lay the tortillas in a single layer on a platter. Top each tortilla with an equal portion of the steak. Top the steak with equal portions of the cheese and then equal portions of the sour cream mixture. Top the sour cream with equal portions of the tomatoes and the scallions. Fold the tacos up and serve them with additional lime wedges and hot sauce on the side.

Makes 4 servings

LOTTA HERB RUB

An herb rub imparts a more sophisticated flavor than the typical dry rub and you have to be careful not to burn it, but your guests are going to be impressed.

> **2 tbsp Morton's Kosher Salt**
> **1 tbsp Sugar In The Raw or other raw sugar**
> **1 tsp chili powder**
> **1 tsp black pepper**
> **1 tsp granulated garlic**
> **1 tsp granulated onion**
> **1 tsp dry mustard powder**
> **1 tsp dried thyme leaves**
> **1 tsp dried basil leaves**
> **1 tsp dried oregano leaves**
> **1 tsp dried tarragon leaves**

In a small bowl, combine the salt, raw sugar, chili powder, pepper, granulated garlic, granulated onion, mustard, thyme, basil, oregano, and tarragon. Mix them well until fully blended. Store in an airtight container in a cool dry place for up to 2 months.

Makes about ⅓ cup (75 g)

Rubbed Rack of Lamb

You can sub chops in this recipe and grill them quickly, but the whole rack of lamb is simple, elegant, and very impressive at the table. Roasted mini potatoes are a great side for this dish.

2 racks of lamb, trimmed, about 2 lb (910 g) total
2 tbsp olive oil
Lotta Herb Rub (page 149), as needed

Preheat the oven to 400°F (200°C). Rub the lamb all over with the olive oil. Sprinkle a liberal coating of the rub on all sides of the lamb racks. Let them rest for 5 minutes.

Place the racks on a baking sheet bone-side down and place in the oven. Cook them for 15 minutes. Flip the lamb racks over and cook them for another 10 minutes, until the racks are golden brown and reach an internal temperature of 135°F (58°C) for medium-rare. Remove the racks to a platter and tent them loosely with foil. Let them rest for 5 minutes. Cut the racks into single or double chops to serve.

Makes about 4 servings

SESAME SEED RUB

This rub is built for rare tuna steaks, but don't hesitate to use it with chicken breasts or pork chops to give them an exotic flavor.

> ¼ cup (35 g) white sesame seeds
> ¼ cup (35 g) black sesame seeds
> 2 tsp Morton's Kosher Salt
> 1 tsp black pepper
> 1 tsp granulated garlic
> 1 tsp granulated onion

In the bowl of a food processor, combine the white and black sesame seeds, salt, pepper, granulated garlic, and granulated onion. Pulse them two or three times, just until the seeds are broken down and the ingredients are combined. Store in an airtight container in a cool dry place for up to 2 months.

Makes about ½ cup (90 g)

Seared Sesame Tuna

I like to cook these just enough to let the flavors of the rub bloom while the tuna stays raw in the center. Have everything ready when the tuna hits the hot pan, because this should be served immediately after cooking. I always serve this on a small bed of greens with wasabi, pickled ginger, and soy sauce on the side.

2 thick ahi tuna steaks, about 2 lb (910 g) total
1 recipe Sesame Seed Rub (facing page)
¼ cup (60 ml) vegetable oil

Cut the steaks lengthwise to make four tuna logs. Place the rub on a shallow plate and press the tuna into it on all sides to coat the logs evenly.

Heat the vegetable oil in a large skillet over medium-high heat. Place two pieces of the tuna in the skillet and cook them for about 20 seconds per side, cooking them on all four sides. Remove the tuna to a cutting board and cook the remaining tuna. When all the tuna is done, immediately slice it all thinly to serve.

Makes 4 servings

TOASTED COCONUT-LIME RUB

This recipe combination comes from my friend, partner in "Cookoff Before Kickoff," and the 2013 World Recipe Champion, Beth Peterson. Beth is really creative in the kitchen, as you can see from this outside-the-box rub. It shows that a rub can be just about anything you like, and I like this!

¼ cup (30 g) toasted unsweetened coconut flakes
¼ cup (50 g) sugar
Zest of 4 limes
1 tbsp Morton's Kosher Salt
⅛ tsp chili powder
A pinch of white pepper

In the bowl of a food processor, combine the coconut, sugar, lime zest, salt, chili powder, and pepper. Pulse them until the ingredients are combined into a medium-fine texture. This rub must be used the day that it's made because of the fresh lime zest.

Makes about ⅓ cup (100 g)

Beth's Grilled Peaches

This is a wonderful grown-up dessert from my friend Beth. I like to add a little vanilla ice cream to the plate, too.

> 4 large just-ripe peaches, halved and pitted
> ¼ cup (80 g) honey
> 1 recipe Toasted Coconut-Lime Rub (page 154)
> Juice of 1 lime
> 2 tbsp honey
> 1 tbsp tequila

Prepare an outdoor grill to cook direct over medium-high heat. Clean the cooking grate thoroughly. Brush the peaches with the honey. Season the peaches liberally with the rub on all sides.

Place the peaches cut-side down directly on the cooking grate. Cook them for 2 to 3 minutes, until they're golden brown. Flip the peaches over and cook them until the second sides are golden brown and the peaches are soft to the touch, another 2 to 3 minutes. Transfer them to a platter and cover them loosely to keep warm.

In a small bowl, combine the lime juice, honey, and tequila. Whisk until they're well blended.

Serve half of a peach to each guest, drizzled with the lime-tequila glaze.

Makes 8 servings

GLAZES

To begin the chapter on glazes, I went to the dictionary

to determine how the rest of the world defines a glaze. The definitions for *glaze* started with a process for fixing windows, and ended with sweet icing for a donut. Both are noble uses of the word, but if you bought this book for home-repair tips or donut topping advice, I'm sorry, but you've made a terrible mistake. Between those two definitions was the one I was looking for. There were a few versions, but the one I was looking for was "a smooth shiny coating applied to a food."

Glazes are essentially sauces that are applied during cooking, and most often at the end of cooking. Barbecue sauce is a great example, and is therefore probably incorrectly named. It should be called *barbecue glaze*. Unlike the do-ahead processes of marinating, brining, injecting, or even rubbing, the glaze is a last-minute application of great flavor. Because of this, glazes also need to be fairly thick so they'll lie temptingly on top of the finished dish. Sometimes the ingredients make a perfect thickness for glazing, and at other times we need a little magic help from a thickener like cornstarch or arrowroot. Some of the recipes here call for brushing with the glaze throughout the cooking. This is simply to add a little extra flavor, but we'll always end with a thin smooth layer on top because using a glaze makes for great appearance as well as great flavor.

Maybe it's the expected appearance of a syrupy texture, or maybe it's the donut factor, but as I looked around I found that many glazes tend toward the sweet side, even for use with meats and seafood. I've never held to that thinking. A little sweetness often works with glazes, but it's just not mandatory. Savory things like vinegars, fruit juices, pureed produce, and even coffee make very good bases for a glaze. I think a glaze can be downright spicy or tangy and still be a great complement to the food it's on top of. Anything that tastes good goes in my kitchen, and since you'll be applying the glaze at the end of cooking, all fully cooked ingredients are on the table.

Feel free to use the glazes here as-is or make them your own. You might also want to use them in combination with the rubs, marinades, brines, or injections in this book.

For simplicity, I've avoided using them in combination here but I surely do it at home and you should, too. The Basic Glaze (page 160) would pair beautifully with a couple of the traditional recipes from the rub chapter and the Chipotle-Honey Glaze (page 178) would be a welcome finish to just about anything.

The glazes in this chapter are all fresh and simple and suited for single use. Fresh ingredients spoil, so for best results don't make them ahead or try to store them. The glazes themselves don't necessarily need to be cooked, but since you will sometimes be applying them to foods that aren't fully cooked, you'll need to discard any leftovers as soon as the food is finished cooking. If you'd like to use some as a side sauce, just divide the batch and set some aside before dipping the brush in. Or simply make a second batch to be used as a sauce.

This chapter begins with a basic and very simple glaze recipe. After that, the more elaborate glaze recipes will have icons next to them suggesting which foods they are best suited for, followed by a complete recipe utilizing the glaze. So have fun mixing, grab a brush, and get glazing!

THE BASIC GLAZE

Simple Barbecue Glaze

This is the simplest of all homemade barbecue sauces, and it goes well with just about anything as a glaze or served on the side. Add whatever flavors you like to make this your own.

2 tbsp butter
¼ cup (30 g) finely chopped yellow onion
1 garlic clove, crushed
1 cup (240 ml) ketchup
½ cup (100 g) packed brown sugar
¼ cup (60 ml) cider vinegar
½ tsp Morton's Kosher Salt
½ tsp black pepper
½ tsp cayenne (optional)

In a small saucepan over medium heat, melt the butter. Add the onion and cook it for 3 to 4 minutes, until it's soft. Add the garlic and cook it for another minute. Add the ketchup, brown sugar, vinegar, salt, pepper, and cayenne (if using). Mix them in well. Bring the sauce to a simmer and adjust the heat to maintain a low simmer. Cook it for 5 minutes, stirring often, until the sauce has thickened slightly. Set it aside to cool before using.

Makes about 1½ cups (360 ml)

PINEAPPLE-MOLASSES GLAZE

The classic combination of pineapple and molasses is the core of this tasty glaze. Fire up the charcoal and the aroma will have you feeling very Polynesian when this one hits the heat.

½ cup (120 ml) pineapple juice
½ cup (120 ml) unsulphured molasses
1 tbsp cornstarch
2 tsp cider vinegar
1 tsp granulated onion
1 tsp granulated garlic
¼ tsp cayenne

In a medium microwave-safe bowl, combine the pineapple juice, molasses, cornstarch, vinegar, granulated onion, granulated garlic, and cayenne. With a whisk, mix them well. Cover the bowl loosely with plastic wrap and microwave it on high for 1 minute. Remove it from the microwave and mix the glaze well. Cook it for another minute, until the glaze thickens. Mix it well. Set it aside to cool before using.

Makes about 1 cup (240 ml)

Pineapple-Grilled Pork Chops

Pork chops topped with these flavors are a real classic. I'd pair this with a big pile of fried rice and a drink served in a coconut.

> 4 bone-in pork chops, 1 in (2.5 cm) thick
> Morton's Kosher Salt
> Black pepper
> 1 recipe Pineapple-Molasses Glaze (facing page)

Prepare an outdoor grill to cook direct over medium heat. Season the chops with salt and pepper.

Place the chops on the grill and cook them for 3 to 4 minutes, until they're golden brown on the bottom. Flip the chops over and brush a liberal coating of glaze over the top, spreading it to cover well. Cook the chops for another 3 to 4 minutes, until the second side is golden brown, then flip them over and glaze the second side. Continue cooking them, flipping and brushing at 1-minute intervals, until the chops are golden brown and they reach an internal temperature of 150°F (65°C). Top each chop with a final thin layer of the glaze. Discard any remaining glaze. Transfer the chops to a plate and tent them loosely with foil. Let them rest for 5 minutes. Serve one chop to each guest.

Makes 4 servings

APPLE PIE RIB GLAZE

Any rib glaze needs a good bit of sweet to complement the savory rib meat, and this one gets it from the flavor-packed apple butter and an extra little hit of cinnamon.

> 1 cup (240 ml) ketchup
> ½ cup (140 g) apple butter
> ¼ cup (50 g) packed brown sugar
> ½ tsp Morton's Kosher Salt
> ½ tsp black pepper
> ¼ tsp ground cinnamon

In a medium microwave-safe bowl, combine the ketchup, apple butter, brown sugar, salt, pepper, and cinnamon. With a whisk, mix them well. Cover the bowl loosely with plastic wrap and microwave it on high for 1 minute to melt the sugar. Remove it from the microwave and mix the glaze well. Set it aside to cool before using.

Makes about 1½ cups (360 ml)

Oven-Cooked Barbecue Ribs

This is a bit of a cheater recipe for ribs, since they're oven-cooked, but it's a tasty one. Feel free to switch to the outdoor grill or smoker. You'll just need to adjust your cooking time to fit your device. These ribs are great served with baked beans and cornbread.

> 2 slabs pork loin back ribs, about 4 lb (1.8 kg) total
> 1 tbsp Morton's Kosher Salt
> 2 tsp paprika
> 1 tsp granulated garlic
> 1 tsp black pepper
> 1 recipe Apple Pie Rib Glaze (facing page)

Preheat the oven to 300°F (150°C). Peel the membrane off the back of the ribs. Trim any excess fat from the ribs.

In a small bowl, combine the salt, paprika, granulated garlic, and pepper. With a small spoon, mix them well. Season the ribs with the spice blend, using one-third on the bone side and two-thirds on the meaty side.

Place the ribs on a baking sheet in the oven. Cook them for 2 hours. Set aside one-third of glaze to be used later as a sauce.

Brush the ribs liberally on the top and sides with the glaze. Return them to the oven for 30 minutes. Brush the ribs again with a liberal coating of the glaze. Raise the temperature of the oven to 400°F (200°C) and return the ribs to the oven. Cook them for 30 minutes more. Remove the ribs from the oven, and tent them loosely with foil. Let them rest for 5 minutes. Cut each slab into three pieces and serve one piece to each guest, with the reserved glaze on the side.

Makes 6 servings

JAVA JUICE

This is a glaze with a big coffee punch and a little kick of cayenne at the end. It might even keep you up at night thinking about how good it was.

1 cup (240 ml) strong coffee

¼ cup (60 ml) fresh orange juice

3 tbsp brown sugar

1 tbsp arrowroot powder

¼ tsp Morton's Kosher Salt

¼ tsp cayenne (optional)

In a medium microwave-safe bowl, combine the coffee, orange juice, brown sugar, arrowroot, salt, and cayenne (if using). With a whisk, mix them well. Cover the bowl loosely with plastic wrap and microwave it on high for 1 minute. Remove the bowl from the microwave and whisk the glaze again. Repeat the microwave/whisking step once or twice more, until the mixture is smooth and has thickened. Set it aside to cool before using.

Makes about 1¼ cups (300 ml)

Java-Glazed Pork Tenderloin

The sweet coffee glaze works beautifully with the flavor of pork tenderloin, which is leaner than a boneless skinless chicken breast. This dish is tasty *and* good for you, so let's keep it that way by serving it with brown rice and green beans.

> 2 whole pork tenderloins, about 2 lb (910 g) total
> Olive oil
> Morton's Kosher Salt
> Black pepper
> 1 recipe Java Juice (page 167)

Prepare an outdoor grill to cook direct over medium heat. Trim any excess fat membrane from the tenderloins. Rub the meat liberally with olive oil, then season it with salt and pepper. Set aside one-third of the Java Juice to be used later as a sauce.

Place the tenderloins directly on the cooking grate. Cook them for 3 to 4 minutes, until the bottoms are lightly browned. Flip the tenderloins one-third of the way over and cook them for another 3 to 4 minutes, until the second sides are lightly browned. Flip the tenderloins another one-third of the way to the last side and cook them for another 3 to 4 minutes, until those sides are lightly browned. Brush the tenderloins all over liberally with the Java Juice. Continue flipping and brushing them every couple minutes until the tenderloins are golden brown and reach an internal temperature of 150°F (65°C). Brush the tenderloins with a final thin layer of the glaze. Discard any remaining glaze. Transfer the tenderloins to a platter and tent them loosely with foil. Let them rest for 5 minutes. To serve, slice the tenderloins and drizzle them with the reserved glaze.

Makes 6 servings

MAPLE-MUSTARD GLAZE

This glaze isn't just for mustard lovers only. It's got a lot of the tangy yellow stuff, but the real maple syrup creates an amazing transition to mellowness.

¾ cup (180 ml) pure maple syrup
¼ cup (60 ml) Dijon mustard
¼ cup (60 ml) yellow mustard
¼ tsp Morton's Kosher Salt
¼ tsp black pepper

In a medium bowl, combine the maple syrup, Dijon mustard, yellow mustard, salt, and pepper. With a whisk, mix them well. Use immediately or cover and refrigerate for up to 1 week.

Makes about 1¼ cups (300 ml)

Tasty Chicken Strips

Chicken strips get all grown-up here and extra flavorful when they get coated with this tasty and simple glaze. I think these are great served with baked sweet potato wedges.

    4 boneless skinless chicken breast fillets, about 2 lb (910 g) total
    1 recipe Maple-Mustard Glaze (facing page)

Preheat the oven to 350°F (175°C).

Cut each chicken breast lengthwise into three equal strips. Divide the glaze into two equal portions and set one aside. Dredge the chicken strips in the glaze, coating them well on all sides. Lay the strips on a baking sheet and place the baking sheet in the oven. Discard the used glaze.

Cook the chicken for 20 minutes. Remove the baking sheet from the oven and spoon half of the unused glaze over the strips. Bake them for 10 minutes more, until the internal temperature of the chicken reaches 160°F (73°C). Remove them from the oven. To serve, transfer the strips to a platter and drizzle them with the unused glaze.

Makes 4 servings

BLACK COKE GLAZE

The quest for fun new ingredients is something that is a constant part of my life, and sometimes they are right there under my nose. Coke is sweet and caramely with a taste that everyone loves, so it works beautifully in this glaze.

2 cups (480 ml) Coca-Cola
½ cup (50 g) Sugar In The Raw or other raw sugar
½ tsp Morton's Kosher Salt
½ tsp black pepper
2 tbsp water
3 tbsp cornstarch
Juice of 1 lime

In a small saucepan over medium-high heat, combine the Coke, raw sugar, salt, and pepper. With a whisk, mix them well. In a small bowl, whisk together the water and cornstarch. Add the cornstarch mixture to the pan and mix it in well. Bring the glaze to a simmer and lower the heat to maintain a simmer. Cook the glaze for about 12 minutes, stirring occasionally, until it is thickened and reduced by about half. Add the lime juice and whisk it in. Set it aside to cool before using.

Makes about 1 cup (240 ml)

Chicken Wings with Black Coke Glaze

Chicken wings hot off the grill are a pretty easy match with just about any tasty topping, and this Coke glaze is no exception. This recipe switches to the oven easily, too. Just lay the wings on a baking sheet and bake them as directed on page 78. Try serving these wings with salty pretzel sticks on the side.

12 whole fresh chicken wings, about 2½ lb (1.2 kg) total
Olive oil
Morton's Kosher Salt
Black pepper
1 recipe Black Coke Glaze (page 173)

Prepare an outdoor grill to cook indirect at 350°F (180°C). With a sharp knife, cut the tips off of the wings, then slash the inside of the wing joints just through the skin. Liberally rub olive oil on the wings, then season them with salt and pepper.

Place the wings directly on the cooking grate. Cook them for 30 minutes. Flip the wings over and cook them for another 30 minutes, until the wings are tender and reach an internal temperature of 180°F (83°C). Transfer the wings to a large bowl. Drizzle the glaze over the wings, and then toss them until they're well coated. Transfer the wings to a platter to serve.

Makes 4 servings

SWEET-AND-SOUR GRILL GLAZE

The timeless combination of sweet and tart comes together in a Zen-like way for this glaze. Your taste buds will be in a very happy place.

¼ cup (60 ml) pineapple juice
1 tbsp cornstarch
¼ cup (60 ml) rice vinegar
¼ cup (50 g) packed brown sugar
¼ cup (60 ml) ketchup
1 tbsp soy sauce
1 tbsp honey
1 tsp sriracha sauce

In a medium microwave-safe bowl, whisk together the pineapple juice and cornstarch. Add the vinegar, brown sugar, ketchup, soy sauce, honey, and sriracha. Whisk them well. Cover the bowl loosely with plastic wrap and microwave it on high for 1 minute. Remove it from the microwave and mix the glaze well. Repeat this process two more times, until the glaze has thickened. Set it aside to cool before using.

Makes about 1¼ cups (300 ml)

Sweet-and-Sour Chicken Thighs

This one is a Dr. BBQ version of sweet-and-sour chicken. The sweet and tangy sauce really comes to life when it's combined with the smoky flavor from the grill. These go really well with stir-fried vegetables.

> 8 boneless skinless chicken thighs, about 2 lb (910 g) total
> Morton's Kosher Salt
> Black pepper
> 1 recipe Sweet-and-Sour Grill Glaze (page 175)

Prepare an outdoor grill to cook direct over medium heat. Season the thighs with salt and pepper on both sides.

Place the chicken thighs directly on the cooking grate. Cook them for 3 minutes, until the bottoms are lightly browned. Flip the thighs over and brush the tops with the glaze. Cook them for another 3 minutes, until the second sides are lightly browned. Flip the thighs over and brush the second sides with the glaze. Continue cooking, flipping, and brushing them at 2-minute intervals, until the thighs are golden brown and reach an internal temperature of 180°F (83°C). Top each thigh with a thin layer of the glaze. Discard any remaining glaze.

Transfer the chicken to a plate and tent it loosely with foil. Let it rest for 3 minutes. Serve two thighs to each guest.

Makes 4 servings

CHIPOTLE-HONEY GLAZE

With this glaze, big flavors come together for an epic battle of sweet versus smoky and spicy. But as with any cooking, when the balance is right, there is a harmonious and delicious ending.

> 8 scallions, white and green parts coarsely chopped
> 4 chipotle chiles in adobo sauce
> ⅓ cup (105 g) honey
> 4 garlic cloves, minced
> ½ tsp Morton's Kosher Salt

In a blender or small food processor, combine the scallions, chipotles, honey, garlic, and salt. Blend them until smooth, about 1 minute. Add 1 tbsp water if the mixture is too thick to blend.

Makes about ⅔ cup (160 ml)

Chipotle-Glazed Chopped Steaks

Regular old ground beef has a whole new look when you make a big oval patty out of it and then top it with a flavorful glaze. It'll never be regular again. I like to serve this with creamy macaroni and cheese.

> 2 lb (910 g) ground round steak
> Morton's Kosher Salt
> Black pepper
> 1 recipe Chipotle-Honey Glaze (facing page)

Prepare an outdoor grill to cook direct over medium-high heat. Form the meat into four balls of equal size. Form each ball into an oval patty, about ¾ in (2 cm) thick. With your thumb, make a small indentation on the center of each patty. This will keep them at an even thickness as they cook. Season the patties with salt and pepper.

Place the patties directly on the cooking grate. Cook them for 3 minutes, until the bottoms begin to firm up. Flip the patties over and brush the tops with the glaze. Cook them for another 3 minutes, until the second sides begin to firm up. Flip and brush them with the glaze. Continue flipping and brushing them every 2 to 3 minutes, until the patties are golden brown and reach an internal temperature of 155°F (70°C) for medium. Top each chopped steak with a thin layer of the glaze. Discard any remaining glaze.

Transfer the patties to a plate and tent them loosely with foil. Let them rest for 3 minutes. Serve one patty per guest.

Makes 4 servings

FRESH HARISSA GLAZE

Harissa is sometimes called the ketchup of Trinidad. There are many unique versions, but they all involve chiles and toasted seeds and are quite spicy. My fresh version is no exception.

4 serrano chiles, seeded and coarsely chopped
2 poblano chiles, seeded and coarsely chopped
½ red bell pepper, seeded and coarsely chopped
4 garlic cloves, crushed
¼ cup (7 g) packed fresh mint leaves, coarsely chopped
¼ cup (60 ml) beef broth
¼ cup (60 ml) olive oil
1 tbsp chili powder
1 tsp Morton's Kosher Salt
½ tsp red chili flakes
2 tsp coriander seeds
1 tsp caraway seeds
1 tsp cumin seeds

In the pitcher of a blender, combine the serrano chiles, poblano chiles, bell pepper, garlic, mint, beef broth, olive oil, chili powder, salt, and chili flakes. In a small skillet over medium heat, toast the coriander seeds, caraway seeds, and cumin seeds, swirling them around the pan often for about 30 seconds, until you smell them beginning to toast. Dump the seeds over the chile mixture. Blend it on high speed for about 1 minute, until smooth. Transfer to a bowl and use immediately.

Makes about 1 cup (240 ml)

Flat-Iron Steak with Harissa

Flat-iron steak is a jewel of the meat case and as good as it gets on the grill. It's tender and tasty, a good value, and is perfect served with crispy homemade french fries.

> 2 USDA Choice flat-iron steaks, about 2 lb (910 g) total
> Olive oil
> Morton's Kosher Salt
> Black pepper
> 1 recipe Fresh Harissa Glaze (facing page)

Prepare an outdoor grill to cook direct over medium-high heat. Cut the steaks into two pieces each. Rub the steaks liberally with olive oil, then season them with salt and pepper. Reserve one-third of the glaze to be used later as a sauce.

Place the steaks directly on the cooking grate and cook them for about 3 minutes, until the bottoms are lightly browned. Flip the steaks over and brush them with the glaze. Cook them for another 3 minutes, until the second sides are lightly browned. Flip them over and brush the second sides with the glaze. Continue cooking, flipping, and brushing them at 2-minute intervals, until the steaks are golden brown and reach an internal temperature of 125°F (50°C) for medium-rare. Flat-iron steaks should never be cooked beyond medium-rare or they will be tough. Top each steak with a thin layer of the glaze. Discard any remaining glaze.

Transfer the steaks to a plate and tent them loosely with foil. Let them rest for 3 minutes. Serve one piece to each guest with the reserved glaze on the side as a dipping sauce.

Makes 4 servings

THAI SWEET CHILI GLAZE

Everybody loves that spicy-sweet pink Asian dipping sauce that seems to be everywhere these days. It's also a top-notch ingredient for glazes and more complex sauces, and I use it often. Here, it gets in the pool with a few other simple Asian ingredients and the taste gets very sophisticated.

> ⅓ cup (80 ml) Thai sweet chili sauce
> 1 tsp Thai fish sauce
> 1 tsp soy sauce
> 1 tsp sriracha sauce

In a medium bowl, combine the chili sauce, fish sauce, soy sauce, and sriracha. With a whisk, mix them well. Use immediately or cover and refrigerate for up to 1 week.

Makes about ½ cup (120 ml)

Bacon-Wrapped Shrimp with Thai Chili Glaze

Wrapping anything in bacon is a good idea as far as I'm concerned. When you add the sweet exotic glaze, they become something totally new . . . and great! These can be cooked on the grill, too. Either way, keep an eye on the shrimp and don't overcook them while you're trying to get the bacon crispy. These are great served on top of a romaine salad.

8 slices thin-cut bacon
16 jumbo shrimp, peeled and deveined, tails left on
1 recipe Thai Sweet Chili Glaze (page 182)

Preheat the oven to 375°F (190°C).

Cut the bacon in half crosswise. Cut a slit into the meaty part of each shrimp and spread them so they'll stand up with their tails in the air. Wrap a piece of bacon around each shrimp in a corkscrew fashion, leaving the tail exposed. Secure the bacon with a toothpick near the tail. Stand the shrimp up in rows on a baking sheet that has been coated lightly with nonstick spray.

Bake them for 15 minutes. Brush the shrimp well with the glaze and bake them for another 15 minutes. Glaze them again and bake them for another 10 minutes, until the bacon is crisp and the shrimp are firm and white. Top each shrimp with a thin layer of the glaze. Discard any remaining glaze. Transfer the shrimp to plates, serving four to each guest.

Makes 4 servings

MARGARITA GLAZE

The classic flavors of everyone's favorite tequila drink transition very well to savory dishes, and this glaze is no exception.

- 3 tbsp tequila
- 2 tbsp Cointreau liqueur
- 2 tbsp fresh lime juice
- 1 tbsp agave nectar
- 1 tsp arrowroot powder
- ¼ tsp Morton's Kosher Salt

In a small microwave-safe bowl, whisk together the tequila, Cointreau, lime juice, agave nectar, arrowroot, and salt. Cover the bowl loosely with plastic wrap and microwave it on high for 1 minute. Remove the bowl from the microwave and whisk the glaze again until it is well blended and thickened. Set it aside to cool before using.

Makes about ½ cup (120 ml)

Baked Margarita Salmon

Salmon takes well to many flavors, but lime and a little agave are as good as it gets. And when you add a little tequila and Cointreau, something really special is coming to the table. If you like to grill your salmon, this would be a great time to do it. I like to serve this Cuban-style, with black beans and white rice.

> 4 skin-on salmon fillets, about 6 oz (170 g) each
> Morton's Kosher Salt
> Black pepper
> 1 recipe Margarita Glaze (page 185)

Preheat the oven to 350°F (175°C). Dry the salmon well, then season it with salt and pepper. Place the pieces on a greased baking sheet, skin-side down.

Bake the salmon for 10 minutes. Brush the salmon with a liberal coating of the glaze. Bake it for another 10 minutes. Brush it with another liberal coat of the glaze. Discard any remaining glaze. Bake the salmon for another 10 minutes, or until it is firm to the touch and just beginning to flake.

Remove the salmon from the oven. Let it rest for 3 minutes. Transfer the fillets to individual plates to serve.

Makes 4 servings

TENNESSEE HONEY GLAZE

This recipe comes from my good friend Marsha Hale of Lynchburg, Tennessee. If you have read any of my previous books, you know that I always include a recipe from Marsha because I like the way she cooks. Marsha is a barbecue girl and a great Southern cook. She works at the local factory, which just happens to be the Jack Daniel's distillery, so she's used the local product here and I am a big fan of that, too.

¾ cup (180 ml) Jack Daniel's Tennessee Honey Whiskey
¾ cup (150 g) packed brown sugar
2 tsp vanilla extract
½ tsp cinnamon
½ tsp ground nutmeg
½ tsp Morton's Kosher Salt

In a medium bowl, whisk together the whiskey, brown sugar, vanilla, cinnamon, nutmeg, and salt. Whisk vigorously until the sugar is dissolved. Use immediately or cover and refrigerate for up to 1 week.

Makes about 1½ cups (360 ml)

Honey Whiskey–Grilled Pineapple

Pineapple grills better than any other fruit, so I use it often and so does Marsha. Leaving the rind on makes a very nice presentation and it's simple to eat around it. You can serve this with a cup of coffee, a shot of Jack Daniel's Honey Whiskey, or you might just want to combine the two.

1 whole fresh pineapple
1 recipe Tennessee Honey Glaze (page 187)
6 big scoops vanilla ice cream

Prepare an outdoor grill to cook direct over medium heat. Slice the pineapple into six rounds about 1 in (2.5 cm) thick, leaving the rind intact. Reserve the remaining pineapple for another use. Brush both sides of the pineapple steaks with the glaze and then place them directly on the cooking grate.

Cook the pineapple for about 2 minutes, then flip it over and baste the top with the glaze. Continue cooking, flipping, and basting it every 2 minutes, until the pineapple is golden brown and soft to the touch, about 10 minutes. Remove the pineapple steaks to individual serving plates and drizzle them with any remaining glaze. Top each with a large scoop of vanilla ice cream and serve them immediately.

Makes 6 servings

INDEX